Becoming a Spirit-Led Mom

QUIN SHERRER & RUTHANNE GARLOCK

HARVEST HOUSE PUBLISHERS

EUGENE, OREGON

The stories presented herein are true and have been used by permission. In certain cases the circumstances of particular events and some names of persons and locations have been changed to protect an individual's privacy.

Cover by Harvest House Publishers, Katie Brady, designer

Cover photo © Digital Vision

BECOMING A SPIRIT-LED MOM
Copyright © 2004 by Quin Sherrer and Ruthanne Garlock
Published by Harvest House Publishers
Eugene, Oregon 97402
www.harvesthousepublishers.com

Library of Congress Cataloging-in-Publication Data

Sherrer, Quin.
  Becoming a spirit-led mom / Quin Sherrer and Ruthanne Garlock.
    p. cm.
Includes bibliographical references (p.   ).
  ISBN 0-7369-1132-4 (pbk.)
  1. Mothers—Religious life. 2. Spiritual warfare. I. Garlock, Ruthanne. II. Title.
BV4529.18.S54 2004
248.8'431—dc22

                                                                    2003014750

Printed in the United States of America

   04 05 06 07 08 09 10 11 12 / BP-KB / 10 9 8 7 6 5 4 3 2 1

This book is dedicated to young moms who
desire to be led by the Holy Spirit in raising their children
and in challenging them to fulfill
God's destiny for their lives.

You are becoming today's Proverbs 31 women.

She is clothed with strength and dignity;
she can laugh at the days to come.
She speaks with wisdom,
and faithful instruction is on her tongue.
She watches over the affairs of her household
and does not eat the bread of idleness.
Her children arise and call her blessed;
her husband also, and he praises her:
"Many women do noble things,
but you surpass them all."
Charm is deceptive, and beauty is fleeting;
but a woman who fears the LORD *is to be praised.*
Give her the reward she has earned,
and let her works bring her praise at the city gate.
Proverbs 31:25-31

Acknowledgments

With special thanks to:

Our children: Quinett, Keith, and Sherry, and Linda, Melody, and Bradley, who have been a source of enormous joy in our lives and a means God has used to teach us so much about himself.

Our grandchildren: Lyden, Victoria, Kara, Evangeline, Ethan, and Samuel, and Amanda, Rachel, Lydia, and Joel, who bring us such delight at this season of our lives, and who represent our hope for the future.

Our husbands: LeRoy and John, whose prayer support and practical help made our task a great deal easier.

Our agents: Ann Spangler and Linda Peterson Kenney, whose creativity helped to birth the idea for this book.

Our editors at Harvest House: Terry Glaspey and Kim Moore, whose help on this project has been invaluable.

All the moms who allowed us to share their stories in order to bring inspiration and hope to a new generation of Spirit-led moms.

Contents

A Helper for
Your Journey as a Mom

*You are controlled by the Spirit if you have the
Spirit of God living in you...For all who are led
by the Spirit of God are children of God.*

—ROMANS 8:9,14 NLT

ave you ever asked yourself, after receiving a note from your eight-year-old child's teacher calling for a meeting to discuss discipline issues, *How am I supposed to handle this?* The note says your Billy started a fight on the playground during recess. But he insists the other kid punched him first—and the other kid is your boss' grandson. Then you groan, *Oh, Lord, how did I get to be the grown-up so soon, anyway?*

You probably feel as though you don't have the world completely figured out—and yet you now have the responsibility of directing young lives. Where can one go to find the answers? If you're like us, becoming a mom makes you more aware of your weaknesses than you've ever been before.

Most moms feel inadequate for the monumental task of rearing their children. Besides the energy needed for meeting a family's practical demands, this high calling requires grace, discernment, patience, wisdom, and sensitivity—qualities which most women, if they're truly honest, will say they lack in sufficient quantities.

But there is an answer. God, who created mothers in the first place, has provided everything you need to parent effectively. It only requires that you take advantage of the incredible source of power available through the Holy Spirit.

Becoming a Spirit-Led Mom is filled with contemporary stories, scriptural examples, and guidelines for prayer to help you apply the power of the Holy Spirit to parenting challenges you face every day. The two of us have walked through many situations like those of the moms whose stories we share. We've struggled with the same negative feelings which may be bothering you— guilt, fear, disappointment, anger, regret, impatience, and despair, to name a few.

While we no longer have young ones living in our homes, we speak to women's groups all over the United States, and the women we meet often share their frustrations as struggling moms. We can identify with them, but we also offer them hope.

We are close to our own children and grandchildren. In fact, I (Quin) have a constant hands-on relationship with all six of my young grandchildren, who live close by. I've visited their schools and know their teachers. I've been to their soccer games. I've sat in pediatric offices, hospital rooms, speech therapy clinics, school board meetings, and Sunday school classrooms. I know their friends and their friends' parents.

I also know that my grandchildren are growing up in a world completely different from the one their parents knew as children, where I could let them walk to school and not worry about their safety. If ever there was a day when moms needed the help of the Holy Spirit in raising their children, it is today in the twenty-first century.

Maybe you feel as I did at one time that, even though you're a Christian, you still struggle with your role as a mother. My children were in elementary and middle school before I even heard that the Holy Spirit was available to me to strengthen, encourage, guide, empower, bring revelation, give spiritual gifts, or love through me. But I quickly discovered I had to ask him *daily* to enable me to become a better mom. You probably will make that discovery too.

How grateful I am that all my children have learned the value of depending on the Holy Spirit to help them parent their little ones. I believe I could have avoided much heartache had someone shared with me earlier this amazing gift. What a difference the Holy Spirit has made in my life!

In contrast to Quin, I (Ruthanne) had a powerful experience discovering the Holy Spirit during my early teenage years. But after graduating from college, when I faced the challenge of becoming stepmom to two daughters, I knew for sure I would need his help and guidance as never before to fulfill such a role. The girls were eight and thirteen when John and I married. Then when our son was born two years later, I faced a new set of problems in blending our family. Of course I made mistakes along the way. But without the assistance of the Holy Spirit, our family wouldn't have the loving relationships we enjoy today.

Now, whenever I speak at women's seminars or retreats, I meet women who are wrestling with the unique problems of being a stepmom. I can empathize with their struggles and assure them that, with the Holy Spirit's help, they can find peace, wisdom, and direction for how to relate to their stepchildren and love them with God's love.

It is our hope that single moms, married moms, and stepmoms—at home full-time or working outside the home—will find encouragement here. Whether you have children still at home, or you're in the process of "launching" your children into their future vocations, we pray the Holy Spirit will equip and empower each of you to take pleasure in the journey you're on and to finish the race with joy.

—*Quin Sherrer and Ruthanne Garlock*

1
I Can't Do This Alone
A Mom's Need for Spiritual Power

So let us come boldly to the throne of our gracious God.
There we will receive his mercy, and we will
find grace to help us when we need it.
—HEBREWS 4:16 NLT

Children. To me the very word sparkles with life and laughter!
From babies to teenagers, children teem with energy.
And each one of them represents a life of potential—for
our Lord and for mankind. Nothing demands that
we lean on the Lord more than parenting.[1]
—ELIZABETH GEORGE

oms know they need help.

At some point in our journey as moms, the daunting task of rearing a child to be a responsible, independent adult—as well as a loving, influential servant of God—hits us full force. It is a sobering reality.

But we can tap into the power of the Holy Spirit to receive wisdom for our problems, comfort for our heartaches, and refreshment for our weariness. When Jesus explained to his followers that he would have to leave them soon, he comforted them with this promise: "I will pray the Father, and He will give you another Helper, that He may abide with you forever—the Spirit of truth…He dwells with you and will be in you" (John 14:16-17 NKJV).

We encourage you to invite the Holy Spirit to empower you to raise your children for God. He can provide the wisdom and help you need—don't fail to take advantage of this gift available to every believer. The Holy Spirit living within you enables you to draw upon his power to deal with every situation in life.

The Holy Spirit Makes a Difference

I (Quin) remember one night when I "lost my cool" before I had learned that I could call on the Holy Spirit's help in a trying situation with my children. Our 12-year-old daughter had a school friend over to spend the night, and I let the girls sleep on the downstairs pull-out sofa. My husband had to be up by 6:00 A.M. to go to work, so I reminded them of that before telling them goodnight.

At 1:00 A.M. I went down and asked the girls to stop giggling and talking. At 2:30 my husband went down and asked them to stop. At 4:00 I went down again. This time I yelled, "Your father has to get up to go to work in two hours! March up those stairs and get into your bedroom—both of you. Now go to sleep."

As the girls meekly went upstairs I crawled back into bed. At last the house was quiet, but I could not sleep. Another voice was keeping me awake. A still, small voice that said, "You were wrong to yell. You lost your patience and you were not a good example. Yes, they were wrong, but so were you. Now go and apologize to those girls."

Thirty minutes later I surrendered to that voice by getting up and knocking on my daughter's bedroom door. "Girls, I'm sorry. I shouldn't have yelled," I said. "You were wrong to talk until so late, but I want you to forgive me for my anger and for yelling." They did, and we hugged one another.

That scene flashes before me often—even after all these years—and it reminds me how important it is for me to rely on the Holy Spirit's help instead of handling matters in my own way.

Not an Easy Role

In our survey of dozens of moms, we asked them to identify the most difficult issues they face in their role as a parent. These are the ones most often mentioned:

- dealing with discipline issues

- coping with sibling rivalry

- coping with their own guilt over mistakes they have made

- trying to instill spiritual values in their children's lives (and often feeling a failure at the job)

- helping their children deal with disappointment in not reaching a desired goal

- dealing with a child's chronic illness or depression

- helping their children fit in with their peer group

- setting kids free to have their own experiences with God

No doubt you can identify with one or more of these issues that moms everywhere wrestle with from time to time.

It's all right to admit you have not achieved perfection...that you have rough edges. Truthfully, we don't know of a "perfect mom" anymore than we know of a "perfect child." But we can have as our goal *becoming* a mom who is sensitive to the Holy Spirit's guidance. Becoming means "to grow to be" or "to come to be." Thus we can say we are *in the process* of becoming a Spirit-led mom.

Sure, there may be days when you feel you're failing at the task. But the important thing is not to focus on your mistakes.

Instead, you can learn from them, humble yourself to ask God—and sometimes your children—for forgiveness, and then give thanks to him for helping you improve until you see more successes than failures.

No Instant Results

Becoming or growing to be a Spirit-led mom isn't instantaneous, as our next story illustrates. I (Quin) met a young mom named Mary when she led the worship at a meeting where I was the guest speaker. She had been a Christian for only six years. Yet her loving, personal relationship with Jesus was evident as she worshiped and played her guitar, literally leading us into the Lord's presence. It was so awesome that I could barely regain my composure to get up and speak.

I learned that Mary grew up in a dysfunctional home where her alcoholic father had abandoned her mother and their three children, and she had only rarely gone to church. Because she identified God with her dad, Mary did her best to "be a good girl" so God would love her. It was a long time before she learned that her heavenly Father loves her unconditionally and she couldn't earn his approval through good behavior.

She had finished college, married, and had a child of her own before she received her first Bible as a gift from a friend. Mary read it with a deep hunger, but still, she often would call this friend and complain about her problems. One day the woman rebuked her: "Mary, you haven't given God authority in your life. You're trying to do everything on your own."

Knowing her friend spoke the truth, Mary knelt down in her bedroom and prayed, "Come into my heart, dear Lord, and cleanse me from all my sins. Wash me clean and change my life. Help me to be a wife and mother who will bring you glory. Show me how to win my family and friends to you. I pray in Jesus' name, amen."

Just about this same time her estranged father needed a kidney transplant, and Mary was a perfect genetic match to donate a kidney. She felt God wanted her to do this, not only as an act of compassion, but as a way to reach him for Jesus. Her prayer was answered when, soon after the surgery, Mary's dad committed his life to Christ.

"I learned right after I became a Christian that I must depend on the Lord for every single decision I make—for every way I react to my husband and children or other family members," she said. Mary, whose three children are now eight, six, and two does several things to maintain her walk with the Lord:

- ❧ She daily reads her Bible, meditates on it, and writes her thoughts in a journal.

- ❧ She keeps contact with a few older Christian women she's asked to mentor her.

- ❧ She stays around other Spirit-led moms. "I try to be with Christian women so that, even on my bad days, I have an example of the right way to respond to my children."

- ❧ She volunteers in the music department and hospitality ministry at her church so that she can use the gifts and talents God has given her.

- ❧ She reads biographies of Christians who have changed the world and stories about composers who wrote the hymns she has come to love.

- ❧ She looks for ways to bring God into everything she does with her children. She says, "When the children get a 'boo-boo,' we stop and pray for healing of that hurt."

Mary's list is not a universal prescription for raising godly children—you can make your own list. There are many simple things a mom can do that will yield eternal results. But the important thing is to seek the help of the Holy Spirit as you relate to your children and try to address their physical, emotional, and spiritual needs.

Needing More Grace

One of the many blessings the Holy Spirit can provide is guidance to help us pray according to the will of God (see Romans 8:26-27). Where family relationships are involved, sometimes human emotions cloud our reasoning. But we can call on the Holy Spirit to help us pray effectively and in line with God's will for specific situations regarding our children and family members. Over the years I (Ruthanne) have come to rely on this wonderful resource.

When I married my husband, John, he was a widower with two daughters, eight and thirteen years old. Their mother's death more than a year earlier had occurred with little warning after a brief illness. Immediately, John had to take the children out of school and move cross-country to live with friends while he established himself in a new job. At the time I met him, the three of them had recently moved into a house of their own, and he was struggling with the challenges of single parenting.

Although I believed God had brought us together, I was not at all prepared to deal with the difficulties I encountered when I became a stepmom. And if it was a struggle for me, surely it was even more difficult for Linda and Melody. The hardest times were when John had to travel and it fell on my shoulders to enforce household rules and make disciplinary decisions. I quickly learned the necessity of asking for God's wisdom for each problem as it arose.

I can still remember waking up one Saturday morning after John had left for a weekend speaking engagement. It was now several weeks after the wedding. Suddenly I felt overwhelmed with fear that I had made a huge mistake marrying John and taking on the responsibility of two daughters. As my mind filled with doubt and guilt, I began calling on the Lord to give me his peace.

The Holy Spirit instantly reminded me of one specific evening after we had become engaged when I was seriously considering breaking off the relationship. I had gone to a chapel service alone and asked the Lord to show me clearly what I should do. By the time the service was over, I felt God's assurance that it was his will for me to marry John and that I must simply trust him to help me with all the adjustments my new life required.

Looking back on that night when I had sensed his clear guidance, I thanked the Lord in advance for giving me the grace, wisdom, and strength I would need to build a relationship with my stepdaughters. I asked him to minister to their emotional needs and to help me love them with unconditional love.

An old hymn that I had learned years before became my declaration of faith. When the going got tough, these words reminded me of God's faithfulness and assured me that his grace was sufficient for whatever I needed:

He Giveth More Grace

He giveth more grace as our burdens grow greater,
He sendeth more strength as our labors increase;
To added afflictions He addeth His mercy,
To multiplied trials, His multiplied peace.

His love has no limits, His grace knows no measure,
His pow'r has no boundary known unto men.
For out of His infinite riches in Jesus,
He giveth, and giveth, and giveth again.

When we have exhausted our store of endurance,
When our strength has failed 'ere the day is half done,
When we reach the end of our hoarded resources
Our Father's full giving is only begun.[2]

—Annie Johnson Flint (1886–1932)

Of course I made mistakes, the greatest of which was not fully appreciating and allowing for the trauma John and his daughters had been through. If I could go back and do some things differently, I would. But I've learned that God can redeem our mistakes in amazing ways and help us compensate for them. Now, 39 years later, I'm very grateful for the loving relationship I have with Linda and Melody, and with their children. They know I pray for them regularly, and they feel free to ask me to pray for them for specific situations. Indeed, God has proven to me that his grace is greater than any problem I ever face.

Remember, whatever hard place you are going through, God can replace ashes with beauty (see Isaiah 61:3).

One mom wrote this as a testimony of her experience:

> I have found tremendous help in daily early morning prayer for my kids and our family—and also through prayer interspersed throughout the day. I have come to view God as the best child psychologist. He made our children. He knows them best, and he has all the answers I need. Sometimes he gives me insights while I'm praying, sometimes through his Word, sometimes through other people (mothers, grandmothers, friends, my husband), and sometimes through the passage of time. But going to him first is essential for me, and then I look everywhere to see his answers.

"Help Me, Lord"

Looking back on past mistakes is a humbling experience. But nothing is wasted in God's economy—not even the heartaches or the times we feel we were failures as parents.

I (Quin) went to the Lord many times admitting, "I can't do this alone. Help, help, help me," as my husband and I tried to bring our children up in "the training and instruction of the Lord" (Ephesians 6:4). We were Sunday school teachers and church leaders when each of us personally asked God to empower us with his Spirit so that we could live more effectively for him. Our children had been in church with us since they were infants, but at the time we made this all-out commitment to the Lord, they were preteens.

Our renewal touched our children too. We began having family devotions around our kitchen table, encouraging our children to memorize Bible passages and teaching them to pray aloud and to keep prayer journals even as we were learning. I remember clearly the time each one stood publicly in a church and invited Christ into his or her heart.

But by the time they went away to college, we realized that peer pressure was greatly influencing them and they were drifting from God. For five years my husband and I prayed diligently for their turnaround. I spent hours searching the Bible to find God's promises for our family. I listened to pastors, church leaders, and more experienced moms. Sometimes I wrote down their prayers and then adapted them and made them my own.

One evening I heard a friend pray this for her four children and thirteen grandchildren: "Lord, keep them from error, keep them from deception, and may they be worthy to stand before you at your coming." I incorporated that prayer into my daily petitions for my children.

Another time, one of my older prayer partners prayed this for my children: "Lord, guard Quin's children from wrong friends, wrong environment, and wrong influences, and bring the right people into their lives." I immediately added that to my daily prayer for them. Also, by paraphrasing Scripture verses, I regularly prayed prayers like this one:

> Lord, your Word says all my children shall be taught of you, and great will be their peace—I claim that promise for each of them. Your Word also says that the seed of the righteous shall be delivered. Thank you, Lord, that I am righteous because of Jesus' shed

blood, and my children are my seed. So I am trusting you to deliver them from every evil thing that has drawn them away from you (see Isaiah 54:13 and Proverbs 11:21 KJV).

During this difficult five-year period, my husband and I would see things in our kids' lives which we knew did not honor God. But with the help of the Holy Spirit, we stood on his promises, persisted in prayer, and asked friends to join us in praying for our children to fulfill God's purpose for their lives. When my son came home on weekend visits from college, I'd sometimes speak a verse of Scripture to him before he started back. "Son, you are a mighty man of God," I told him once. I found other Scriptures I could paraphrase, often inserting his name, as I prayed various verses for him.

All three of our children returned to the Lord in the same year. Since then, each of them has attended Bible school and been involved in overseas assignments from smuggling Bibles into China and helping build a church in Africa to ministering in Europe, Israel, Asia, and the United States.

Even though looking back is sometimes painful, I see God's faithfulness through all my mistakes. I realize now I should have prayed more and preached less...offered more encouragement instead of criticism...listened more to what they were really trying to say instead of judging too quickly. I should have watched their friendships more closely.

I was learning, experimenting, and trying to hear the Lord's voice myself in those days. But today I can say that God has far surpassed what I could ask or think when he answered our prayers for our children.

Last year my son sent me a Mother's Day card with this verse on it:

Mothers are made by tackling challenges,
overcoming difficulties,

and struggling with extraordinary problems.
I made you what you are today, Mom!
Happy Mother's Day.[3]

At the bottom of the card he wrote:

Mom, I figure as much as you've written about me, I
have to take some of the credit—the rest is the Lord's.
Thanks for being you!
Love, Number One Son

When I received that card, I remembered one night after he'd
finished college when he called to ask us to forgive him. His dad
and I both said yes, but amazingly, we cannot recall what it was
he asked forgiveness for. The Holy Spirit's eraser sweeps things
clean! Today I cherish memories of all the happy, fun times of his
childhood. When we ask him, the Lord truly does help us to
adjust our attitudes and heal our relationships.

The Challenge for Single Moms

Becoming an effective, hands-on mom is indeed a formidable
task—but for single moms it is even more difficult. By the beginning of the year 2000, the number of single mothers in the U.S.
had increased to ten million.[4] And the majority of these moms
now must work outside the home. Michelle is one of them.

After escaping an abusive marriage, she and her toddler,
Stuart, moved into her parents' home until she was settled into
a job and earning enough to maintain an apartment for the two
of them. Because her ex-husband contributes very little financial support, managing her money with only a moderate income
is one of Michelle's greatest concerns.

"I have to depend on God to show me how to stretch dol-
lars, find clothes bargains, and locate free cultural events where
I can take my son," she said. "Most of all, I need the Holy Spirit
to help me be effective in mothering my only child without

smothering him. I also have to guard against giving in to Stuart or spoiling him just because he doesn't have a dad nearby."

Michelle readily admits she can't parent without God's help. Her day begins at 5:30 each morning when she reads her Bible for ten minutes while still in bed. Then she prays briefly, asking God to guide her through the day before heading for the shower. She has lunches to pack, her son's preparation for school to oversee, bills to mail, and the challenge of getting out the door in time to drop Stuart off at daycare and make it to her office by 7:30 A.M. Then she faces a busy day on the computer and telephone, interfacing with dozens of people at her job.

Stuart, now seven years old and in second grade, goes to day-care before and after school. In the afternoons he plays with about two dozen other children until his mom picks him up before the daycare closes at 6:00 P.M.

As soon as she gets home, Michelle kicks her shoes off and collapses across the bed for a short nap while Stuart watches a Christian video. Then she prepares supper for the two of them, makes sure he does his homework, and reads to him before tucking him into bed.

Saturdays find her cleaning house, washing clothes at the laundromat, shopping for groceries, running errands, and some-times hunting through thrift shops for clothes. She attends a church known for its youthful congregation, and once a month she helps with Stuart's Sunday school class. Besides finding much-needed spiritual support from the single moms' meetings at her church, Michelle occasionally meets other moms at a park so their children can play together while the women visit.

"Single parenting isn't easy," she says. "During the day I find myself praying often, asking God for wisdom to be a good mom and also a good employee when I have to deal with an irate cus-tomer on the phone.

"As a mother, I have to depend on the Holy Spirit to help me make right choices for my son. One day when Stuart was playing outdoors with a friend I heard a string of obscenities coming from his playmate's mouth. I ran outside and explained to them why such 'trash talk' was totally unacceptable. The other boy said he was sorry, but moments later he was cursing again. I had to tell Stuart he can no longer play with him. Of course, this is hard because there are so few children in our apartment complex who are my son's age."

But there are positive male role models in Stuart's life. He plays with his boy cousins, spends time and sometimes overnights with his granddaddy, and frequently goes with his uncle to softball and soccer games. Michelle feels they are blessed to be able to live near family members who are a good influence on her son.

"Discipline is probably the hardest issue," she laments. "Getting Stuart to obey the first time I tell him something has been the most difficult. Once on the way to a birthday party I asked him to put down a sharp writing pen he was playing with because of the possible danger to him if I had to stop suddenly. He did not obey, even when told a second time. I held my tongue and prayed about what to do. *Just take him back home*, I felt the Holy Spirit directing me. So I turned the car around and drove home. He was shocked and disappointed over missing his friend's party, but I explained to him that there are penalties for disobedience. After that incident he was much more willing to listen and obey.

"It's really hard sometimes to make decisions like this, but the Lord gives me creative ideas just when I need them. Years ago I invited the Holy Spirit to be my teacher, and I depend on him to help me with single parenting and every other area of my life."

Always Learning, Always Leaning on God

These words from Glenda Malmin help us see the challenge of motherhood from a broad perspective:

> The motherhood journey has a beginning but no ending. Once you open yourself to it, your life

becomes a continuum throughout the life of your child. The realization that you do not give birth to mere human flesh, but rather to an eternal soul, settles into your spirit in an awe-inspiring way.

Motherhood also has changing seasons. There will be days of joy, when you feel like there is no child quite like yours. And there will be days of frustration and exhaustion, when you are sure there is no child quite like yours...I have discovered that the seasons, as well as the emotions, of motherhood vary. I've also discovered that whether you are a single mom or a married mom, your journey has dimensions of commonality with all mothers.[5]

We are all at different stages—still learning, still depending on the Holy Spirit to teach us. As you go through the various phases of rearing your children, always remember—in good times and bad—that you can commit your children into God's hands and trust him to reveal his love and faithfulness to them.

He wants to empower us to become effective, influential Christian moms. But we can't reach our full potential of effectiveness as parents if we don't engage the power of the Holy Spirit to help us. Let's stop right now and thank God for our children and ask for his guidance in rearing them.

Prayer

Lord, I offer thanks for the children you have entrusted to my care:___(name them)___. I know your plans for my children are for good and not for disaster, and to give them hope and a future (see Jeremiah 29:11 NLT). Lord, I desire to instill in them a love for you and the desire to walk in your ways, but I feel so inadequate for the task. Please send the Holy Spirit to instruct and enable me. Help me to love my children with your love, and give me your wisdom as I face the challenges their future will bring. Thank you for redeeming my mistakes and imparting your blessings to me and my children. Amen.

Scriptures for Meditation

"But the Counselor, the Holy Spirit, whom the Father will send in my name, will teach you all things and will remind you of everything I have said to you" (John 14:26).

"May the God of hope fill you with all joy and peace as you trust in him, so that you may overflow with hope by the power of the Holy Spirit" (Romans 15:13).

"Haven't you yet learned that your body is the home of the Holy Spirit God gave you, and that he lives within you? Your own body does not belong to you. For God has bought you with a great price. So use every part of your body to give glory back to God because he owns it" (1 Corinthians 6:19-20 TLB).

"We have everything we need to live a life that pleases God. It was all given to us by God's own power, when we learned that he had invited us to share in his wonderful goodness. God made great and marvelous promises, so that his nature would become part of us. Then we could escape our evil desires and the corrupt influences of this world" (2 Peter 1:3-4 CEV).

"God has said, 'I will never leave you; I will never abandon you.' Let us be bold then, and say, 'The Lord is my helper, I will not be afraid. What can anyone do to me?'" (Hebrews 13:5-6 GNT).

2

Power for Your Fears

Finding Peace That Lasts

*You will keep in perfect peace him whose mind is steadfast,
because he trusts in you. Trust in the LORD forever,
For the LORD, the LORD, is the Rock eternal.*
—ISAIAH 26:3-4

*Fear is only empowered to the degree we yield to its deception.
Fear steals our power by tricking us into believing its lies.
Imaginary fears can become real if we believe in them.
Even the most unfounded ones can alter the course of our lives
and in turn change our destinies. The destination for the
children of Israel was the promised land, but they
forsook God's promises to embrace their fears.
They placed their faith in their fears. In doing this
they chose the devil's lies over God's truth.[1]*
—LISA BEVERE

*C*ountless moms struggle with their private fears, even though peace is God's promise to us. Some of the primary fears women have shared with us include fear of: the future, rejection, failure, financial lack, abandonment, disease, pain, death, and losing a loved one. Often our most troubling fears are those concerning our children.

In this chapter we want to point you toward the peace that only God can provide. His peace is available to us despite the noisiness of toddlers, the busyness of school-aged children, the internal turmoil of discord with a teenager, or the potential dangers our grown-up children face in today's chaotic world.

Actually, fear and faith start at a common point: Both believe something is going to happen. Unhealthy fear believes something bad—such as a sudden calamity—will happen. Faith, on the other hand, believes something good will happen, or that God can bring a positive result out of a disappointment. Most of us are a mix of these two qualities, but we can choose which one we allow to dominate our thoughts and actions. The more we choose to walk in faith with our minds steadfastly fixed on God, the more his peace becomes our anchor.

At a very practical level, fear can be useful. When my (Ruthanne's) strong-willed son was two years old, he would try to pull away from me when I took him out of the car, not wanting me to hold his hand as we crossed the parking lot. That is, until the day he ran ahead of me and almost got hit by a car as we headed into the supermarket. After that episode, he had a healthy fear of cars and would willingly take hold of my hand. The challenge is to teach our children how to take reasonable precautions against danger while instilling in them a trust in God that will protect them from unhealthy anxiety.

It's probably safe to say that fear is one of the most potent weapons our enemy, the devil, uses against moms. Our adversary assails us with tormenting thoughts which paralyze our faith, feed our minds to imagine the worst, overwhelm our emotions, and cause us to focus on the problem instead of the solution.

Many times in his teaching and in his prayers, Jesus gave warnings or made references to this adversary. Yet he *always* gave his followers the assurance of his provision: "The thief [that is, the devil] comes only to steal and kill and destroy; I have come that they may have life, and have it to the full" (John 10:10).

Acknowledging the source of fear is one step toward overcoming it. Whenever we sense the enemy is stealing our peace by filling us with fear, we can bring our thoughts under control by focusing on the promise Jesus gave: "In this world you will have trouble. But take heart! I have overcome the world" (John 16:33). He is the source of peace, not of fear.

In the midst of our anxious, fear-filled world, God's message to us is this: "Don't fear!" Over and over throughout the Scriptures, God tells us not to be anxious, afraid, worried, or terrified. As Spirit-led moms, we need to heed that message every day of the year.

"What if?" Scenarios

I (Quin) will never forget my first real encounter with fear as a new mom. My baby was six weeks old, and because my regular doctor had been called up for military duty, I had to travel with my mom to a large nearby city for my daughter's first check-up. I had already lost a baby to miscarriage, and I was naturally fearful about this newborn.

"Take off the baby's clothes and then hand her over to me," the nurse said. I reluctantly surrendered my daughter to a strange woman in white who disappeared behind a closed door—to take my child for measuring and weighing, I supposed. Other nurses came and took naked babies from other mommies, and none of us were allowed to follow. I just about panicked.

"What if they bring me back the wrong baby?" I asked Mom in a very serious tone.

"I don't think they can fool me. I will know my granddaughter whether she is dressed or not," she answered with a chuckle.

It sounds pretty silly now, but I was so full of fear. I sterilized as many things in our house as I could, determined that this baby was not going to get any diseases and die on me! I'd lie awake at night listening to her breathe.

As a mom I can identify with many other fears. Over time I went through other wrenching experiences, such as surrendering my youngest child to an eye surgeon when she was only eight months old, waiting in an emergency room for the doctors to tell me the extent of injuries a child had sustained in an auto wreck, trying to bargain with God when I feared our son was missing in the Gulf of Mexico after surfing, praying against cancer when our college-age daughter had to have an ovary removed, fighting anxiety and the temptation to beg, "Please come home!" when a bomb was found on our oldest child's doorstep while she was living in Israel.

When the children were growing up, I would sometimes allow my imagination to go wild. What was going to go wrong next? I could come up with a lot of possibilities. But we made it through dangerously high fevers, childhood diseases, and broken bones. And later, broken engagements and broken promises. Eventually I came to see I had to trust God to see me through one situation at a time. But my, how the mind can play tricks on us if we give in to the "what if?" scenarios as I used to do.

This is good advice for moms to follow:

> Give your entire attention to what God is doing right now, and don't get worked up about what may or may not happen tomorrow. God will help you deal with whatever hard things come up when the time comes...Meet today's problems with today's strength. Don't start tackling tomorrow's problems until tomorrow. You do not have tomorrow's strength yet. You simply have enough for today.[2]

Enforcing Victory over Fear

Our friend Leah shared with us how she came to a place of daily trust after a years-long struggle she had with fear.

This struggle began with her frequent illnesses as a child, causing her mother and grandmother to be overprotective. An uncle and some of her cousins, picking up on her fearfulness, would taunt her with outlandish threats until she would run into the house and hide under the bed.

Her fears carried over into her marriage, tormenting her with thoughts that her husband might be unfaithful to her while he traveled on business trips. Or that an intruder might break into their apartment while she was at home alone. After the birth of her two daughters, it seemed her anxiety only intensified.

Finally she shared with her husband how miserable she was to be living in almost constant fear. "He helped me understand that the best defense is a good offense," she said. "If I was in a defensive mode, it was too late—the enemy already had the upper hand. I took the Scriptures as my offensive weapon, especially Psalm 91. A footnote in my Amplified Bible says, 'The rich promises of this whole chapter are dependent upon one's meeting exactly the condition of these first two verses.'"

> He who dwells in the secret place of the Most High shall remain stable and fixed under the shadow of the Almighty [Whose power no foe can withstand]. I will say of the Lord, He is my Refuge and my Fortress, my God; on Him I lean and rely, and in Him I [confidently] trust! (Psalm 91:1-2 AMP).

Leah said she had to focus on truly dwelling in God and declaring, "Lord, I choose to trust you and to rely upon you." Then she would go to the places she'd always had to check repeatedly—the front door, the closets, the shower curtain. She would proclaim aloud the promises in Psalm 91 and thank the Lord for sending his angels to protect her and her household.

As Leah was winning her victory over fear, she realized that her older daughter showed signs of becoming a fearful child just as she had been. She began using Scripture as her offensive weapon.

"I am careful to teach my girls the importance of caution without instilling fear," she told us. "We've taught them that when they feel afraid they must say, 'There's no fear, in Jesus' name.' Sometimes Becky wants me to say it for her, but I insist that she must say it for herself. We've also taught them 1 John 4:4: 'Little children...greater is he that is in you, than he that is in the world' (KJV)."

Whenever Leah feels fear rising in her, she uses God's Word against it, and her daughters, now teenagers, do the same. "This is our greatest weapon to enforce the victory we've seen in our family," she said.[3]

Faith and Trust Dispel Fear

Like Leah, Dottie is a mom whose fears came from the experiences of her past. Just before she was born, her father had been drafted and sent off to fight in the Vietnam war. He returned a broken man, spending many years in the mental health wards of veterans' hospitals.

Although she became a Christian as a young girl, in her heart Dottie grew more and more angry with God because of what had happened to her dad. During a college communion service one night, she wept and uttered a short prayer: "Lord, I invite the Holy Spirit to come to help me, correct me, change me. I yield to what you want for my life."

That prayer launched her on a spiritual journey, and a few years later she married Sean, who became a military chaplain. Although she was trying to serve the Lord, Dottie still struggled with her inner anger. Then, when Sean began showing signs of depression, fear became her constant companion. Anything associated with fear found ways to assault her thoughts.

Some days Sean was so badly depressed she had to dress him for work. On other days, when she read Scriptures and sang hymns over him, it was as though she had injected him with medicine and he functioned more normally. Over time, prayer finally brought him through to victory over depression.

Dottie's first child, Gena, was born with no sign of problems. But at four months of age her growth slowed and she became hyperactive. For the first 13 months of her life, the baby didn't sleep for more than two hours at a time, night or day. This not only taxed Dottie's strength and nerves, but it fed more fear into her thoughts. Would her baby die?

Doctors finally determined that Gena had contracted lead poisoning from the old water pipes in the military base housing and suggested Dottie's family use bottled water. Gradually she put on weight, but the hyperactivity remained. Remembering how peace had come to her husband during his struggle with depression, Dottie began singing hymns and reading aloud certain Bible verses over her baby. That seemed to be the only thing that would calm her.

Soon after their second child was born, Sean was transferred to a base in Asia where air pollution was out of control. Both children began suffering from asthma. In one two-week period Dottie had to rush Gena to the emergency room ten times. Again, fear attacked her, and a sense of having no control over the situation stirred up her anger. Could her children continue to survive in this environment?

Dottie's deliverance from anger and fear was a process, like peeling an onion, she says. Daily she would ask the Lord to search her heart and change her. In the meantime she memorized Scriptures, learned more effective ways to pray, and invited older women to mentor her.

When doctors told Dottie her child's hyperactivity and asthma would no doubt be permanent, she began praying against their prognosis. She paraphrased Colossians 2:14 (KJV) into a prayer: "Blotting out the handwriting of ordinances that was against Gena, which was contrary to her, Jesus nailed it to his cross."

She also prayed that Gena, like Jesus, would grow in "wisdom and stature, and in favor with God and men" (Luke 2:52). Every night she spoke a blessing over the child and taught her prayers to pray. She explained to Gena that Jesus' blood was shed for her sins and for anything that tried to rob her of her peace.

When Gena told her mom she saw scary faces on the wall of her bedroom, Dottie taught her to say, "The blood of Jesus can wash off anything, so faces, you have to go." Even at age three, she'd do this and later tell her mom they were gone.

In kindergarten, when she heard a bad word or saw something scary in a movie, she would say, "The blood of Jesus can wash that off my mind and my heart."

"I was teaching her and our other two children that they can be overcomers and not victims," Dottie said. She continues to pray this blessing prayer over them nightly:

> The LORD watches over you—the LORD is your shade at your right hand; the sun will not harm you by day, nor the moon by night. The LORD will keep you from all harm—he will watch over your life; the LORD will watch over your coming and going both now and forevermore (Psalm 121:5-8).

The family now lives where there is almost daily sunshine and clean air, so the children's asthma symptoms have diminished greatly. Gena's hyperactivity is completely under control without her taking medication. Recently a woman complimented Dottie about her eight-year-old daughter, saying, "She is so calm and well-mannered." Dottie was thrilled, because she remembers the remarks people used to make: "My, what an overactive little girl you have!"

How does a mom deal with her own sense of fear and yet provide assurance of peace to her children? Dottie realized her children could easily "catch" her fear, so she began quoting God's Word to them and was careful about what she said and how she responded to their questions. We have included some of her favorite verses at the end of the chapter.

Fear of the Unknown

Talk about a reason to fear! One morning during the writing of this book I (Quin) sat in a room full of women—mostly moms—whose military husbands had been deployed to the Persian Gulf region or were still in training for frontline defense. Many of these women would soon be kissing their husbands goodbye, not knowing for sure when or if they'd see them again.

Their fears were very real. Military wives face a different set of circumstances than some of us. "How do you cope?" I asked the woman sitting next to me that day.

Darcie admitted she had lots of fear. She's a 28-year-old mom with three sons ages two to six, and another due in three months. Not only is her husband in the military, so are her dad and her brother. She herself is in the reserves and could be facing a call to duty if she weren't pregnant.

"The *unknown* is what causes me the greatest anxiety," she admitted. "Of course I have a concern about my husband shipping overseas, even of him being killed. I've asked myself lots of times how could I possibly raise four boys alone. Would the money he leaves be enough? I've been a Christian since I was 13 and should know better than to give in to this fear. So I am learning to live one day at a time. I believe concentrating on God's Word is the only antidote to fear. I am teaching Scriptures to my young sons so they won't give in to fear, either."

Darcie and her husband read the Bible together regularly, and she's asked him to help remind her of the verses they commit to memory. Right now she is concentrating on Psalm 116:7: "Be at rest once more, O my soul, for the LORD has been good to you."

This is another one of her favorite sections of Scripture. Jesus is talking to his diciples:

> See what I have given you? Safe passage as you walk on snakes and scorpions, and protection from every assault of the Enemy. No one can put a hand on you.

> All the same, the great triumph is not in your author-
> ity over evil, but in God's authority over you and
> presence with you. Not what you do for God but
> what God does for you—that's the agenda for
> rejoicing (Luke 10:19-20 THE MESSAGE).

Throughout the New Testament we see that peace usually refers to the inner tranquility of the Christian whose trust is in Christ. The peace that Jesus spoke of was a combination of hope and quiet trust in God. But as the woman in our next story discovered, many times such peace comes in the wake of many trials.

Faith That Moves Mountains

When my (Quin's) friend Kathe Wunnenberg learned that the baby in her womb had so many problems it could not possibly survive after birth, she had already been on a bittersweet journey. She had struggled with infertility, then adopted a baby boy, and then been surprised by this pregnancy after 15 years of marriage. Despite her fears, she was trusting God to heal her baby—but even if he did not, she promised herself and him she would still trust her Creator.

As Kathe tried to cope with the painful prognosis that death was imminent for her baby, a friend told her she was hosting a Labor of Love shower for her. Yes, her situation was unique, but her friends wanted to encourage her with an uplifting day of singing, prayer, food, and surprises. When she showed up and saw nearly 50 women amid streamers, balloons, and banners, she was overwhelmed.

That afternoon Kathe shared words of faith with her friends that surprised even her: "We all face mountains in our life journey," she said. "They block our view, they paralyze us with fear and hopelessness, they stand as a monument of what we can't control. But the pathway to faith and victory is to focus on the

Mountain Mover and not on the mountain." Looking about the room through tear-filled eyes, she knew God had moved mountains in many of these women's lives.

One friend quickly went outside to retrieve something that had been in her car's trunk for several months. She came back into the room and, to reaffirm what Kathe had just said, gave her a gray T-shirt with the inscription: "Mountain Movers...faith that moves mountains. Matthew 17:20." Kathe was touched beyond words.

"Mountain Movers" became her labor-and-delivery motto. She ordered T-shirts with that inscription to give to friends who came to the hospital to be with her. She even hung a T-shirt on the wall in the hospital, and during the long night of difficult labor she focused on its message. Later she wrote about it:

> God was faithful to the motto He had given me. He moved my mountain of fear and replaced it with faith. He used my situation to soften hospital workers' hearts, moving them closer to Himself. He moved multitudes across the country to pray for us. And even though my son didn't survive, God gave me the privilege of being his mother and the faith to believe I will see him again in heaven...
>
> I had believed God would physically heal our child and had publicly proclaimed His ability to perform a miracle...My journey of faith wasn't an easy one. At times I was flogged with fear, stoned with doubt, chained to expectations, and imprisoned with tears. But God sustained me, guided me safely through, and taught me to surrender. It was a process of letting go of every fear, doubt, expectation, and tear, one by one, and relinquishing each one to Him. I suffered, yet endured.[4]

She not only buried this son that she had carried to term, but including miscarriages, Kathe lost four children in all. Later, when I met her at a writers' conference where I was teaching, she was pregnant again. Naturally, she was concerned about her pregnancy. When the class ended, she asked if my prayer partner, Kerry, and I would pray for the health of her baby. Of course we would.

We asked God to give her a safe delivery and a healthy baby. We also prayed against any fear of death the enemy might try to bring upon Kathe during the remaining days of her pregnancy. It was one of those times when I knew the Holy Spirit was leading me as to how to pray, and I felt great confidence that the Lord would answer our prayers.

A few months later, Joshua was born, "healthy and a fighter," according to Kathe. She finished her second book on grief and then found out that at age 42 she was pregnant again. When this son was born, she named him Jordan, "as a testimony to my crossing over to the land of peace, milk, and honey," she wrote me.

I have beside my desk a picture of a smiling Kathe with her three sons, including Jake, her 12-year-old adopted son, Joshua, and Jordan. Above the photo Kathe wrote: "Here is living proof of God's power at work."

Fearing for Our Children's Future

We mothers know well the importance of praying prayers of protection for our children from the time they are small. But concern about dangers they may encounter after they've left the nest and gone out on their own can tempt us to worry even more than we did when they were under our watchful eye. We have to stand against fear and continue to pray in faith as the Holy Spirit leads us.

When my (Ruthanne's) son transferred to a university in New York City for his last two years of study, I stepped up those protection prayers—especially praying Psalm 91 over him.

Occasionally I received reports that assured me my prayers were not in vain.

One day Bradley called to say he had been walking across campus to class that morning when all of a sudden he heard a loud crash and screams. He turned around to find that an entire window—the steel frame with the glass panes—had fallen from an upper floor of a building that was being refurbished. When a group of students several paces behind him saw it fall and barely miss hitting him, they screamed and ran up to see if he'd been hurt. Bits of shattered glass were in his hair and on the back of his coat, but he was unharmed. I believe beyond any doubt that God had appointed an angel to protect Bradley that day (see Psalm 91:11).

Another time, he had just bought a supply of tokens at the subway station near his dorm, and he still had in his hand $10 in change. Just then a young man came up and asked for help, saying he needed to go visit his sick grandmother and had no money. Bradley reached into his pocket for a subway token to give to him, when the guy suddenly grabbed the $10 bill out of his hand and ran out of the station.

Outraged, my son took off after him, yelling, "Hey, you can't have that!" He caught up with the guy and snatched the money back. Then he ran back to the turnstile, put in a token, raced to the platform, and jumped on a train that "just happened" to be there at that moment with the doors open. Bradley waved at the would-be thief caught on the other side of the turnstile as the train pulled out of the station.

When I warned him that he needed to be extra careful because of the neighborhood he was living in, he had an answer for me. "Well, Mom, here's the problem—you raised me to be nice to people, so I was just doing what you taught me to do." He admitted that the school administrators had warned students to be on guard for this kind of activity in the area, and he became more wary after this incident. But he agreed with me that God was watching over him, and he was grateful.

Every praying mom probably has stories like this—and no doubt there are many other times when God protected our children when they weren't even aware of it. I believe the Lord allows us to learn of such instances to remind us of his faithfulness, to give us opportunity to offer thanks to him, and to encourage us to remain faithful in prayer.

Fear can indeed be overcome when we invite, or allow, God to bestow his peace and tranquility upon us as we walk through life's difficult circumstances. He longs to empower us with faith as we learn to surrender every fear to him, one day at a time.

Prayer

Lord, I want to be set free from fear. Help me to claim the promises in your Word and to trust you for everything that happens in my life and in my children's lives. Help me to instill this trust in my children so they will not be overcome by fear. Whenever I'm tempted to be fearful, give me your strength to repel it. I commit myself to you—believing that you will never leave me nor forsake me. Thank you for giving me new hope and the courage to rise above my doubts and fears. Amen.

Scriptures for Meditation

"When I am afraid, I will trust in you. In God, whose word I praise, in God I trust; I will not be afraid. What can mortal man do to me?" (Psalm 56:3-4).

"But the Counselor, the Holy Spirit, whom the Father will send in my name, will teach you all things and will remind you of everything I have said to you. Peace I leave with you; my peace I give you. I do not give to you as the world gives. Do not let your hearts be troubled and do not be afraid" (John 14:26-27).

"For you did not receive a spirit that makes you a slave again to fear, but you received the Spirit of sonship. And by him we cry, 'Abba, Father.' The Spirit himself testifies with our spirit that we are God's children. Now if we are children, then we are heirs— heirs of God and co-heirs with Christ" (Romans 8:15-17).

"We are people of flesh and blood. That is why Jesus became one of us. He died to destroy the devil, who had power over death. But he also died to rescue all of us who live each day in fear of dying" (Hebrews 2:14-15 CEV).

"Casting the whole of your care [all your anxieties, all your worries, all your concerns, once and for all] on Him, for He cares for you affectionately and cares about you watchfully...be vigilant and cautious at all times; for that enemy of yours, the devil, roams around like a lion roaring [in fierce hunger], seeking someone to seize upon and devour. Withstand him; be firm in faith" (1 Peter 5:7-9 AMP).

"There is no fear in love. But perfect love drives out fear, because fear has to do with punishment. The one who fears is not made perfect in love" (1 John 4:18).

3

Power for Your
Weaknesses and Strengths

Learning to Depend on God

I can do everything through him who gives me strength.
—PHILIPPIANS 4:13

*God could collect a mountain of my own words and stack
them against me on judgment day. How the evil one
likes to remind me of those words, especially the
words I've said to my children.*

*But I have also confessed that Jesus is my Lord.
And because of those words, I have been acquitted—pardoned,
cleared, exempted from judgment, forgiven, reprieved.
Like my computer delete button that clears errors,
confession clears careless words.*[1]
—MIRIAM NEFF

eaknesses. We all recognize we have some: impatience, a sharp tongue, a tendency to worry, spiritual sluggishness, and overcommitting ourselves, just to name a few.

But don't be too hard on yourself. You have some strengths too! And you can ask for the Holy Spirit's help in using them effectively.

As you begin to assess your strengths, you can, in the process, allow God to work through you in new ways. You can avoid the hazardous path of self-reliance by learning to depend on the Holy Spirit to help you use your strengths under his direction.

At the same time, you can trust him to reinforce your weaknesses. Character development, it's called! We want to encourage you to cultivate godly character traits as you deal with your weaknesses in your role as a mom.

"The fruit of the Spirit is love, joy, peace, patience, kindness, goodness, faithfulness, gentleness and self control. Against such things there is no law" (Galatians 5:22-23). This listing of the fruit of the Spirit contrasts sharply with the much longer list called "the works of the flesh" (verses 19-21). Clearly, the qualities we desire to exhibit in our lives can only come through the work of the Holy Spirit in us. One Bible commentator puts it this way:

> The Holy Spirit always produces a nobler standard of work than the flesh. And such an outcome does not come through human power but from a holy Presence pervading the life. The fruit of the Spirit is character rather than conduct—being rather than doing...
>
> Another aspect of fruit is that it does not exist for its own sake or even for the sake of the tree, but for the support, strength, and refreshment of those who care to gather the fruit.[2]

Love Replaces Anger

Yes, we need the work of the Holy Spirit to produce this fruit in our lives, but our cooperation also is required. I (Quin) remember a time when I was losing my self-control with one of my kids. At that moment, I couldn't have told you whether I even liked—let alone loved—this child.

But suddenly the Lord dropped into my mind a Scripture reference. I kept hearing over and over: "Romans 5:5, Romans 5:5." I looked it up and read, "The love of God has been poured out within our hearts through the Holy Spirit who was given to us" (NASB).

This was my answer. I could ask God to fill my heart with his unfailing, unconditional love through the Holy Spirit. I stopped right then and asked him to do that.

Something miraculous happened. Love replaced anger. I used that verse many times during my children's growing-up years. I'd literally reach my right hand up to heaven and pray, and then place that hand over my heart as an act of receiving his love. The prayer usually went like this: "Lord, pour your love into my heart! Please do it now because I can't even find my mommy love. Come, Holy Spirit. I invite you and expectantly anticipate that you will fill me with overflowing love for my child. I praise and thank you for it, amen."

When I cooperated with the Holy Spirit, he was able to do in me and through me what I could not do in my own strength. This really sums up the essence of what it means to be a Spirit-led mom. The following story is another example.

Walking Free

Lisa Bevere, a mother of four, describes her struggle to overcome anger and her decision to finally surrender to God the control of her life. Once when her two-year-old had not obeyed her orders to take a nap, she snapped. Just as she was about to react in a horrible manner, the terror in his eyes made her realize she had crossed a threshold in anger she could not afford to let go any further. As she shares in her book *Out of Control and Loving It*, she then did something all moms can do: She took ownership of her problem.

> I threw myself down on my living room floor and wept
> until I had no strength left. At that moment I realized
> the problem did not lie with my parents, my husband,
> my children, the pressures, my upbringing, my ethnic
> background, or my hormones—it was with me. Those
> things were pressures, but I alone was responsible for
> my reactions to them.
>
> I wept because I doubted I could ever be free from
> this anger. It had been a part of me for so long that
> I excused it as a weakness or a personality flaw. Now
> I had come face-to-face with it. No longer was it
> draped in excuses. I saw it for what it really was—a
> destructive, self-willed force that I had allowed to
> control me.[3]

On the floor that afternoon Lisa cried out to God for help:
"God, I don't want this anymore. I will no longer justify it or
blame it on anyone else. Forgive me, Lord." At that moment she
felt the weight of sin and guilt lifted from her. She had humbled
herself, acknowledged the anger for what it was, repented, and
renounced it. Immediately she sensed God's forgiveness and his
promise to equip her to overcome this area of weakness.[4]

But, as you perhaps have discovered, "walking out" our
freedom on a daily basis is not always easy. It may take a while to
break the old patterns we've practiced for years and, instead, to
yield to the work of the Holy Spirit to change and renew us.

One of the first things God asked Lisa to do was to call her
mom and ask for her forgiveness. She made the call, and through
tears, mentioned a very painful incident from the past. As they
talked, her mom asked Lisa to forgive her for the hurt she had
caused in that situation, saying it had weighed upon her for years
too. Mother and daughter forgave one another and then prayed
for one another. Lisa says her confession released both of them.
She admitted she was sorry for the breach she had allowed to

exist between them all those years because her mother truly is a wonderful woman.[5]

Patience

Patience—another aspect of the fruit of the Spirit which the Lord wants to see in our lives—is a trait most of us feel we have in short supply. Yet it is in the midst of circumstances which test our patience that the Holy Spirit can help us to cultivate this quality. Karen's experience is one example.

When this young mom and her husband learned that their son, Jason, was born with Down's syndrome, of course they felt disappointment. But after a few days they began to feel God's peace. "Yes, we grieved in the beginning," Karen said. "But then I concluded that my husband and I, with God, were in this child-rearing business together."

She didn't ask God "Why?" Nor would she have considered an abortion had she known of the birth anomaly ahead of time. She accepted this child as God's gift and trusted him to help her develop the patience to become the best mom she could be.

"I wouldn't trade Jason for a normal boy because he is who God made him to be and nobody else," Karen wrote. "It goes back to the old saying, 'God doesn't make junk.' He's perfect in God's eyes. Parents of a Down's child are told to expect him to perform at the very lowest end of the scale, so everything above that is a great accomplishment. Every little thing Jason does is a triumph. You do work hard in therapy for those triumphs, but there's great joy in them."

This Spirit-led mom and her family have prayed Jason through many physical hurdles, including colostomy surgery and then the reversal of the procedure a year later. Unlike many congenital disorders, Down's syndrome is not a terminal condition. The child can live a relatively normal life at home, and in many cases go to school, learn to read, and hold a job.

"What is so refreshing to me is their innocent, childlike qualities," Karen said. "All they say and do, even as they get older, is precious to the Lord. We 'normal' people lose that as we grow up. All the answers to prayer we've seen in Jason's life have increased our faith."

Karen taught her son at home for his first nine years, but now she's having him evaluated to see if he can attend regular school. She recognizes that he needs interaction with other children and hopes this may also improve his social skills.

As a mom to a child with special needs, Karen would be the first to tell you that it requires a lot of patience to parent both Jason and his two siblings. The other children have their own "mommy needs" too, so sometimes Karen feels stretched. But she sees her motherhood role as God's happy assignment to her.

Cultivating the fruit of patience often requires the virtues of waiting, enduring, persevering, and seeking serenity. But when we remind ourselves of just how long-suffering God has been with us, it helps us to exhibit patience toward our children.

Joy

The good news about joy is that it doesn't depend on happiness or ideal circumstances. One definition we like is: *Joy is an attitude of gratitude.* Because joy is mentioned more than 200 times in the Bible, it must be pretty important to Father God. We can learn to experience this fruit of the Spirit regardless of our victories or defeats.

I (Quin) once had a pastor who had us host a "joy party" for any member of the church who had lost his or her job or who was in a financial crisis. We would take food to that person's home and have a big cookout, assure the member's family that we were committed to praying for them, and then bless them financially by collecting a love offering.

Our pastor based his idea on this verse: "Consider it pure joy, my brothers, whenever you face trials of many kinds, because you know the testing of your faith develops perseverance. Perseverance must finish its work so that you may be mature and complete, not lacking anything" (James 1:2-4).

Few of us consider it joy when we're facing trials. But do we want to be mature in our faith? Of course. We quickly discover that the maturing process brings many opportunities to exhibit joy in the face of adversity. This true joy can bubble up inside of us, even if our child is making poor grades, the water pipes in the house freeze and break, or our husband gets laid off his job. You can add whatever scenario challenges you most.

I (Ruthanne) remember one particular weekend when I had to deal with one crisis after another until it became almost comical. My husband was out of town for a Sunday speaking engagement. In fact, it often seemed to me that his going away for a weekend would almost guarantee that some kind of crisis would occur.

Late Saturday evening I went down to the basement to wash a load of diapers. My son was about 14 months old at the time—and this was before disposable diapers were easily available or affordable. I started the washing machine and went back up to work in the kitchen, but a few minutes later I smelled something burning. Running downstairs, I discovered the washing machine motor had caught fire. I unplugged the machine and managed to get the fire out, but the diapers were still unwashed. There was nothing else to do but wring them out by hand and wait until the next day to find a Laundromat.

The following morning I drove the girls to church for their Sunday school classes, checked Bradley into the nursery, and went scouting for a Laundromat. I found one not far from the church and put the diapers in a washer, and then I decided to go to the morning service and come back on the way home to put the diapers in the dryer. No one was around when I left the place. But when I returned about an hour and a half later with the kids in tow, the machine was empty. The diapers had been stolen.

Now my problem was to find a store open on Sunday afternoon where I could buy a new supply. In the town where we lived at the time, almost no stores were open on Sundays. I finally found a drugstore open and had enough money to buy a dozen diapers to get me through until Monday. By then John would be back home to deal with our nonfunctioning washing machine. You can imagine my response when John called home that afternoon to see how things were going!

No one enjoys experiencing such frustration, but I did rejoice that the house didn't catch fire and that God helped me get the diapers I needed. Even in trying times, we can know joy because he is on the throne.

I (Quin) had a friend whose child named Joy was the same age as my oldest little girl. Only my friend's daughter was autistic. Volunteers went daily to help the child learn to crawl. I was just one of dozens who would get down on the floor alongside little Joy to help her do her patterning exercises.

Early one morning while it was still dark I received a call that Joy was missing from her bed. Her parents didn't know how long she'd been gone. "Pray, please pray," her distraught mother begged. I drove to my friend's house praying all the way. God seemed to drop his assurance in my heart that the child was not hurt. I shared that with my friend and told her we had to have hope and joy in this difficult situation. We waited and prayed while firefighters combed the nearby palmetto thickets. Just after daybreak they found her hiding safely behind a tree.

Immediately this verse came to mind: "Weeping may last for the night, but a shout of joy comes in the morning" (Psalm 30:5 NASB). We had a prayer meeting right then to thank God for his protection over Joy. And we did a little shouting!

Peace

What mother doesn't want peace? Especially around five o'clock in the afternoon? Peace can be described as a serene calmness, the absence of strife. It is possible to experience such peace even in the midst of chaos. But only Jesus can give us inner peace of mind, soul, and spirit when our hearts are troubled.

When we asked moms how they find a place of peace, we heard these responses:

- I call a "time-out" at my house so I can have at least 15 minutes of quiet. I ask the children to color, read, or do something that will give them some "down time."

- I try to take a short rest on the couch while the kids do activities that are not loud. Afterward I spend the amount of time I used to rest to do something they like—playing a board game with them or going outside to play ball.

- I play a soothing Scripture tape or music CD while I prepare supper to allow the Lord to help me enter into peace, even though I must continue working.

- I send the neighborhood kids home to their own moms and call mine inside for a preplanned activity that they can do alone while I take a break.

- I've typed up a lot of Scriptures and put them on laminated cards that deal with the various areas where I am weakest. The cards are in alphabetical order, so I can grab the ones on peace when that's what I need.

Here's a Scripture that several moms told us they like: "May the Lord of peace himself give you peace at all times and in every way" (2 Thessalonians 3:16).

Talk about trying to find peace! I (Quin) read a story about Dale Evans that I shared with my daughters, hoping it would give them inspiration as they raise their own children. Dale—the busy wife of Roy Rogers—had seven children at home and was having trouble finding a quiet time and place to pray. She decided that the giant boulders honeycombed with hidden nooks behind her barn would be the perfect place. Surely she'd feel close to God there.

But sitting among the rocks, she'd hear only her own thoughts. "Why isn't Linda eating? Is Dodie napping or getting into mischief?" Then she'd feel guilty for not praying, and God seemed a million miles away. Finally, she went on a silent retreat at a convent up in the mountains. There God spoke to her, *Don't look for me here. For you, I am in the noise and the bedlam and the peas on the floor.* That's where Dale said she found him—right at home in the midst of all the day's busyness.

In her kitchen she kept a little loaf-shaped box with Scriptures which she called her "daily bread." She would wait for a free moment, maybe while the oatmeal simmered on the stove, and draw out a verse and say it aloud until she had memorized it. She learned she didn't have to go to the mountaintop or even hide among the rocks to talk to God or to find his peace. She recognized that he was beside her every hour of every day.[6]

Yes, busy mom, you can find God even in the noise and bedlam and the peas on the floor. You can ask him to shower you with his peace right there—a serenity that frees you from anxiety and instills a quietness of soul.

Spirit-led moms have ample opportunity to bring their weaknesses to the Lord. Keeping our hearts clean so our prayers will be answered is anything but easy (see Mark 11:25-26 NASB). Does it seem that God brings sandpaper people into your life—those abrasive personalities who bring out the worst in you? For me (Quin) it was usually a teacher who seemed to have a grudge against my child. Or a neighbor who didn't seem to care that her child picked on mine.

When someone has offended me, I tend to plead, "Oh, God, change her, change him..." only to hear the Holy Spirit whisper that he wants to change me instead. Or I want to scream, "God, get this person out of my life!" And he says, "Not until you can love him as I do."

Blessing Your Enemies

I (Quin) had a friend I'll call Janice who learned to apply a Bible principle to a "sandpaper person" in her life. She and her husband enjoyed going to their son's basketball games, and Don counted on their support. Afterward, the family liked to sit around the kitchen table and share about the events of the game.

But another parent who always sat in their cheering section seemed to dislike their son immensely. Whenever Don made the slightest mistake, the man would scream, "Hey, Don, Mr. Stupid...got brains in your feet, kid?"

Once Janice's husband became so mad he left the game, knowing if he stayed he would punch the man in the face. Finally, he stopped going to Don's games altogether.

"My son was being humiliated. My husband was angry. I could think of nothing to do but pray," Janice told me. "I remembered a Scripture verse that says we should bless those who curse us, and pray for those who mistreat us. That man was cursing my son with his words. So I prayed, 'Lord, in the name of Jesus, I choose to forgive this man. I ask you to bless him. Bless him real good, Lord. Just keep on blessing him! Amen.'" (See Luke 6:28).

The next weekend Janice went alone to the out-of-town game. The man who always yelled at her son saw her. "Mind if I sit here?" he asked, turning into the row where she was. "Other parents from our team will probably sit in this section too," he added.

Janice hesitated. Let him sit beside her? Was he serious? Then she remembered her blessing prayer.

"Go ahead," she said, nodding her approval.

As the game progressed, Janice noticed the man was acting quite differently. Only once did he let go with a string of critical remarks about Don's performance. Turning to Janice he said, "Oh, I'm sorry. I've got to learn to keep my mouth shut and control my temper."

The "sandpaper person" she had prayed for, and asked God to bless, was now apologizing for yelling at her son!

"When Jesus taught us to bless those who persecute us, he knew it was to bring about a change—both in us and in them," Janice said. The result? The man eventually stopped yelling at any of the players, and at out-of-town games he became her protector.

Janice began to apply that Scripture to other situations in her life when she was prone to judge or get mad—even with her three children. I imagine each of us could find opportunities to purposely bless someone to let that person know we think he or she has worth and value—especially our offspring.

Blended Families Face Opportunities

Perhaps one of the hardest adjustments a couple must make is when they bring children from a prior marriage into a new family relationship. Overlooking the weaknesses in your mate's children is a gigantic challenge with so many different personalities involved.

When Saundra and Nick were married, they made a blended family which included two daughters—her five-year-old and his seven-year-old. They agreed they wanted more children. Saundra had become a Christian just before they said "I do," and in her heart she decided divorce would not be an option. She would never bail out of this marriage.

Of course no marriage is an easy street without bumps, detours, and potholes. And blending a family has its own set of challenges. "When we married we decided to call the children 'ours' and do our best not to show favoritism," Saundra said. "But that isn't easy to do, and it certainly is not painless."

She soon realized that when her first marriage failed, she had made the mistake of becoming "best buddies" with her daughter. Now she needed to switch her role back to a mom-daughter one and allow her new husband to correct little Dawn. Saundra had to guard her heart, grit her teeth, and determine not to interfere. She says these were the challenges she had to face:

- allowing someone else to discipline her child

- dealing with the other parents of each of the children

- trying not to repay evil with evil to former spouses

- accepting her husband's child as her own

Saundra and Nick established their home with Christian principles, and all of them attended church together. They had three other children, and today all five are actively serving the Lord.

"I think commitment to the marriage is the best thing you can do for yourself personally, and for the children," Saundra said, looking back over their 29-year marriage. "God has blessed us and we are thankful."

Giving Up Your Expectations

Audrey is another mom who worked at blending a family. She had a son of her own when she married Carl, a widower with four young children he was raising alone.

"You have to learn the wisdom of allowing the Lord to capture your heart," she told us. "Then you are able to walk out the difficulties of life—especially when you consider all your own weaknesses."

Her first challenge was her stepchildren's reluctance to accept her and her son into their home and as a part of their family. "Carl was a relatively new Christian too," Audrey said. "Since the Lord had told me this was the man I was to marry, I just assumed I would be able to handle a new family on my own. But I had a hard time relating to and communicating with his children; and now it was almost impossible to spend as much time with the Lord as I had done before. Really, the first seven years we were just trying to obey the Lord as we struggled to blend all those personalities."

One way she coped with the pressure was to write in her journal. "I could tell God all the yucky things that I felt inside, and it seemed to clear my conscience," she said. "I didn't have to say them out loud to anyone. I gave him my offenses, asked his forgiveness, and then walked away without guilt, cleansed because of Jesus' death."

Financial pressures plagued them constantly. They had two more children and still lived in a house with only 1300 square feet. "We haven't gone hungry, but we have done without a lot of things other people consider necessities," she admits.

When Carl's children were in middle school and high school, they were extremely active in sports—soccer, hockey, football, basketball, softball. So the entire family went to every game. Audrey decided to homeschool their two young daughters so they would be able to stay up later at night and enjoy the games, and not have to get up early to go to school. She feels this was one of the best decisions she and Carl made.

In retrospect, Audrey realizes her life would have been easier had she received professional counseling both before and after her second marriage. "I was not fully equipped to handle this assignment God privileged me to carry," she said. "Also, I wish we had worked more on communication skills so I could have understood what each child truly felt or believed. Sometimes you have to give up your expectations of a perfect family, perfect marriage, and picture-perfect house, and trust God with his better plan for your life. He can take our scrambled eggs and make a delightful omelet."

Each mom has a choice to learn to listen to God's voice, follow as he directs, and allow the Holy Spirit to help her through the maturing process. No one said it would be easy, but the rewards are enormous.

Anne Graham Lotz says this of her own experience:

A long time ago I gave God all of my time, 24 hours a day, and then I let Him give it back to me and show me how to spend it...

I think we women have a unique ability to have an especially intimate relationship with the Lord. From that, we can be a source of blessing to our husbands, children, church and friends. Jesus meets the deep needs of personal satisfaction and fulfillment. He is the only One who really knows you, loves you, accepts you, has a plan for you and gives you the guidance and counsel you need.[7]

What a joy it is to know that when we yield to the ways of the Holy Spirit to help us become mature, fruit-bearing Christian moms, we can see our weaknesses diminish and our strengths be used by the Lord to bring blessing to our families.

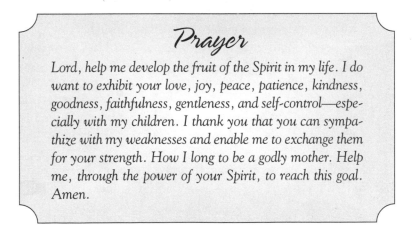

Prayer

Lord, help me develop the fruit of the Spirit in my life. I do want to exhibit your love, joy, peace, patience, kindness, goodness, faithfulness, gentleness, and self-control—especially with my children. I thank you that you can sympathize with my weaknesses and enable me to exchange them for your strength. How I long to be a godly mother. Help me, through the power of your Spirit, to reach this goal. Amen.

Scriptures for Meditation

"'Not by might nor by power, but by my Spirit,' says the LORD Almighty" (Zechariah 4:6).

"Love is patient, love is kind. It does not envy, it does not boast, it is not proud. It is not rude, it is not self-seeking, it is not easily angered, it keeps no record of wrongs. Love does not delight in evil but rejoices with the truth. It always protects, always trusts, always hopes, always perseveres. Love never fails" (1 Corinthians 13:4-8).

"But he [the Lord] said to me, 'My grace is sufficient for you, for my power is made perfect in weakness.' Therefore I will boast all the more gladly about my weaknesses, so that Christ's power may rest on me" (2 Corinthians 12:9).

"I have strength for all things in Christ Who empowers me [I am ready for anything and equal to anything through Him Who infuses inner strength into me; I am self-sufficient in Christ's sufficiency]" (Philippians 4:13 AMP).

"For we do not have a high priest who is unable to sympathize with our weaknesses, but we have one who has been tempted in every way, just as we are—yet was without sin" (Hebrews 4:15).

"Little children, let us not love [merely] in theory or in speech but in deed and in truth (in practice and in sincerity)" (1 John 3:18 AMP).

4

Power to Discipline with Love
Establishing Godly Boundaries

Don't keep on scolding and nagging your children, making them angry and resentful. Rather, bring them up with the loving discipline the Lord himself approves, with suggestions and godly advice.
—EPHESIANS 6:4 TLB

Discipline derives from the root word disciple and it means "to teach." It's a positive, proactive approach that focuses on teaching children appropriate behavior. On the other hand, punishment means to "chastise or correct." It negatively addresses misbehavior after it has occurred. Parents who confuse these two concepts apply a lot of punishment with little or no discipline—and everyone's unhappy.[1]
—TERESA A. LANGSTON

The proper discipline of children requires parents to have godly wisdom, not to mention a large dose of patience. Almost every day they must deal with questions. How do you help your child understand the importance of living within healthy boundaries? Which form of punishment is suitable for this specific child? When is it appropriate to exercise "tough love"? How do you deal with a rebellious teen?

The biblical concept of discipline has both a positive side (instruction, knowledge, and training) and a negative side (correction, punishment, and reproof). Discipline actually means "to train by instruction."[2]

Yet disciplining is perhaps one of the most frustrating tasks a mom must undertake. When my (Quin's) kids were little, it was a fairly common practice for children to be told they'd have to wait until Dad got home to get their punishment. That put unhealthy fear and dread in them and didn't help them deal head-on with their bad behavior. Gradually I learned I had to be firm and issue "time outs" when rules were broken. If it was a big infraction that required Dad's input, I would explain that we'd have to wait and talk about it later.

As I mentioned earlier, I sometimes yelled at my children and then was ashamed afterward. But I determined that, with God's help, I would learn to exercise my parental authority without losing my self-control. How to do that was obvious: We needed to set practical boundaries and guidelines for our children.

My husband and I wrote out a list of what was permitted in our household and the type of behavior we expected from the children—including chores, curfews, and the practice of good manners. From time to time we discussed these in detail with the kids and posted them on the refrigerator door just in case they forgot. We also let them know what was not permitted. I don't remember calling too many "time outs" after they realized I was serious about expecting obedience.

Every Friday evening Dad looked at their charts to see which things they had checked off that they'd done right that week, and then he rewarded them with an agreed-upon amount of money or a special treat or outing. They looked forward to their reward money and usually went skating at our church's gym with their friends afterward.

Our son's favorite pastime, however, seemed to be to tease his sisters. He'd thrust a big green frog in their faces, sending them on a screaming rampage. Or he'd chase the youngest one's much-loved duck to the pond behind our house. To him it was humorous.

To his sisters it was not. They'd run in the house shouting, "Mother! He's got another frog. Stop him." To tell the truth, sometimes it was hard not to laugh at the things our "fun child" thought up to do.

I don't mean to imply that there were never times when our children's infractions were serious enough to require Dad's disciplinary action. There were! But they knew Dad would talk with them alone, and if they needed correcting, he'd do it with love and understanding.

By trial and error I learned what I believe is the bottom line for child-rearing and applying discipline: You must seek God's direction for the individual child as well as for each circumstance you face.

Sometimes, instead of correction or discipline, the best course of action is to react with compassion and understanding. But we need the Holy Spirit's help in making these strategic decisions.

Listening to the Holy Spirit

Marie, a mom with a teenager and a ten-year-old, is learning the importance of seeking guidance from the Holy Spirit in disciplining her children—two girls with very different personalities who are six years apart. Amber, the firstborn, is a high achiever who is the student body treasurer at her school, has lots of friends, always makes top grades, and excels in drama and sports.

Christie, a laid-back fourth-grader who is not nearly as competitive as Amber, tends to feel overshadowed by her talented big sister. Marie became concerned when she noticed that Christie had a tendency to exaggerate the facts when telling a story or reporting on something that happened in school or at church.

One afternoon after Christie arrived home from school, mother and daughter were sitting on the steps in their entry hall, talking. As Christie began relating an incident that had happened that day, Marie knew she was stretching the truth and decided that now was the time to address this problem. But before she opened her mouth to quote a Scripture and tell her daughter how important it is to be truthful, Marie sensed the Holy Spirit's check. She waited for a moment and heard a still, small voice saying, *Why don't you ask her what's really going on in her heart? There's a lot of insecurity there.*

Instead of scolding Christie, she put her arm around her, drew her close, and said, "Sweetheart, what's happening at school? What is it that's upsetting you?"

Christie immediately burst into tears and buried her head in her mom's shoulder. "Oh, Mom, I feel so ugly," she sobbed. "My nose is too big and my ears stick out...and my teacher doesn't like me as much as she does the other kids in my class..."

Marie realized that Christie's exaggeration was her way of compensating for the insecurity she felt when compared to her big sister and her friends and classmates. It was a heartbreaking moment for this mom who herself had contended with feelings of inferiority for most of her life. She knew it wouldn't help for her to try to convince the child that the things she had said about herself simply weren't true—it was time for her to learn a spiritual lesson.

"You know, Christie, it's the enemy—the devil—who tells you those things and makes you feel ugly and inferior," Marie said, wiping her daughter's tears. "God doesn't look at you that way at all, and he doesn't compare you with other people. He has created you for a special purpose, but the devil wants to keep you from fulfilling that purpose by lying to you. No matter how hard you try to win people's approval, that voice will still taunt you and try to make you feel you just can't measure up."

As Marie showed compassion for her daughter and identified with her feelings, a new bond of closeness began to develop between them. She's more sensitive now to finding ways to boost Christie's self-esteem and remind her that God loves her just as she is, and that he has a wonderful future in store for her.

"I want her to learn early on that she can avoid years of misery and comparing herself with others, as I have done," Marie said. "Every day I pray, 'Lord, if there is something I'm missing here with Christie, please show it to me.' This summer I'm going to spend extra time with her exploring her talents and interests—and as her confidence improves, I think the problem of her exaggerating things will disappear. I'm so grateful for the Holy Spirit's help in dealing with this issue while the window of opportunity is open."

Looking back, many of us can probably identify incidents with a child where offering a hug and a sympathetic ear might have done more good than our well-intentioned discipline. Marie's example is a reminder that the Holy Spirit can help us deal with a child's deep needs in a positive way that will have life-long results.

Elizabeth loved her role as a mom to two toddlers, but she faced a new challenge when her third child, Rebekah, was born with seemingly boundless energy and a loud, high voice. "Our first two had never climbed up on top of the dining room table, but Rebekah did," she said. "I didn't want to constantly reprimand her because she was so active. So my husband and I began praying, 'Lord, redirect Rebekah's energy and use it for your glory!' God has answered that prayer, and today, as a teenager, she's dedicated to serving the Lord."

In some cases, though, a mom may hold back from applying needed discipline and training because of her own insecurities. But this too-lenient approach is not in the child's best interests.

Taking Responsibility as a Mom

When Jan became the stepmom of ten-year-old Stacy, she had an irrational fear about disciplining the child when she needed it. "I was so insecure and afraid of being rejected. I didn't want to lose her respect and love," she said. "But finally I sat down with Stacy and gently explained that it was now my responsibility to help her to grow up and become the woman God created her to be."

During a heart-to-heart talk the two decided that even during times when they may disagree with one another, they would show respect and never raise their voices. As she sought the Lord for wisdom and guidance in dealing with disciplinary matters, Jan became more comfortable with correcting Stacy. And their relationship became closer.

When children disobey or show a lack of self-discipline or respect for others, parents must apply discipline—right then! "It is not my desire to make you unhappy," one mom we know told her son when she corrected him. "But my job is to help you become a young man who can make wise choices now and later on, and I'm just doing my job."

The Bible is full of admonitions about discipline (see some of them at the end of this chapter). You might want to memorize one or two of these verses to help you when you talk to an erring child about your responsibility to help instruct him in the ways of the Lord.

Don't Ignore Warning Signs

I (Ruthanne) recall one Friday morning when our son was in high school. I had an unsettled feeling that something was not quite right. I had had my prayer time earlier that day, and my husband had left on time to take Bradley to catch the bus for school. But as I went about my household chores, this sense of uneasiness—what I call my "spiritual radar alert"—became more intense. Finally, I knelt beside the bed I had just made. "Lord," I prayed, "I don't understand why I have such a strong feeling that something is wrong, but I'm asking you to please reveal whatever has been hidden. If the plans we've made for this weekend need to be changed, show us what to do. Thank you, Lord, for your guidance and wisdom. Amen."

My husband and I had registered for the faculty retreat at the Bible school where he was teaching, and we had agreed that Bradley could have a friend stay at the house with him that Friday night. But shortly after I had prayed, the phone rang. It was the clerk in the attendance office at our son's school.

"Mrs. Garlock, I'm calling to check on Bradley's absence from school today. We were told that he is ill, and he wasn't in his first or second period classes."

"No, Bradley is not sick," I replied. "He left home on time to catch the school bus. Can you check to see if he's in his third-period class?"

She put me on hold to check, which gave me a few seconds to pray again and ask the Lord to show me what to do. She came back on the line and said, "No, he's not in third-period class either."

By this time I had a hunch about what might be going on. "Would you mind checking to see if these students are in school today?" I asked, and I gave her two or three names of Bradley's friends.

In a moment she was back. "No, those students are also absent today. Someone called in and said they were sick."

"Hmmm, that's very interesting," I said. "I think I know where these kids might be. Thank you—I really do appreciate your calling me about this."

"Oh, you're welcome," the woman said. "I've been so busy this week I haven't had time to make my usual attendance calls. But today things have slowed down, and your son's attendance slip was on top of the stack."

A coincidence? No, I'm sure that phone call was a direct answer to my prayer.

Now, what was I to do with this information? I felt the Holy Spirit prompt me to phone a store at a shopping mall where one of Bradley's friends worked. When the young man answered I said, "Greg, this is Mrs. Garlock. I'm calling to ask whether you've seen Bradley this morning?"

He was shocked to hear from me. "N-No, ma'am," he stuttered, "I haven't seen him."

"Well, I have a feeling that he just might come by there in a little while," I said. "If he does, please tell him to call home immediately."

When John came home for lunch and heard what had transpired, we immediately agreed it wasn't a good idea for us to go away that weekend. Just then the phone rang.

"Mom, you called?" Bradley asked when I answered. "How did you know where I was?"

"Never mind. Stay where you are," I said. "Your dad is coming to pick you up, and our plans for the weekend are canceled. We'll talk about it when you get home."

Riding back in the car, Bradley was frustrated. "My friends cut school all the time and they never get caught!" he fumed. "How does Mom find out these things?"

"Well, Bradley," John answered, "all I know is that your mom talks to God a lot—and God also talks to her."

"Yeah, I know. That's the scary part," he said glumly.

Looking back, I wonder how many other times the Holy Spirit tried to get my attention about a matter with one of our children and I was too preoccupied to pay attention. If we truly want to be Spirit-led moms, we need to keep our awareness level high so we don't miss the Holy Spirit's promptings.

Bad Behavior Doesn't Mean Bad Child

Children are bound to express anger and disappointment when they're being corrected. Bradley was upset that we had spoiled his plans for the weekend, and we were disappointed that we missed the faculty retreat. We simply had to ask the Lord to help us keep our own frustration in check and to give us his wisdom in communicating with our son.

When punishing a child, it's important that you explain to him that you are addressing the bad behavior. The child is not bad—it was his bad choice that led to the wrong behavior. He must understand that the punishment is a consequence of his behavior.

Author Teresa Langston says this cause-and-effect form of discipline "means that every time your children don't follow the rules, specific consequences result. To this principle, you can add incentives. These are rewards for following rules, and they add a positive dimension to the discipline process." She suggests these guidelines as a parent's best bet:

1. Identify the behavior.

2. Formulate a concrete rule.

3. Attach a specific consequence.

4. Follow through without comment.

5. Reward good behavior.[3]

First-Time Obedience

"We have a rule at our house of first-time obedience," Joyce told us. "Disobedience results in a spanking or additional chores, depending on the offense. I know some people don't believe in spanking children, but we do it once in a while. We use a ruler rather than our hands for this, but we also let our children know we love them unconditionally. I guess the worst thing we deal with right now, with six little ones, is teasing. We want them to show respect to one another, and we try hard to see that they do. So teasing usually gets them more chores, like washing dishes."

Joyce says she often finds herself praying, "Lord, I don't understand this child. I need your wisdom and insight into his personality, his way of learning, his reasons for teasing his sister. Help me to see him as you see him. Help me respond to him as you would."

Brenda Armstrong is a single mom who found herself reacting to her children in negative ways when they reached their teens. She realized she had to change her style of discipline as her children grew and changed. "Teens have a way of expressing attitudes that can cause overreactions in weary parents," she wrote. "I had to learn to stop and pray when that feeling of reacting started. When I did this, God gave me the strength and perspective to handle the situation properly."[4]

Most of us can think back to times when, because of fatigue or feeling the pressure of too many things to do, we overreacted and made a bad situation worse. All moms could benefit from following Brenda's example of praying over each disciplinary issue, rather than reacting emotionally.

Just Say No

As moms learn to rely on the Holy Spirit's guidance, they can begin to discipline with love in a constructive way. Sometimes we learn by observing other godly mothers, like the mom in our next story.

My (Quin's) friend Linda had a typical 11-year-old son who sometimes would argue with her. She had observed our pastor's wife, Jackie Buckingham, in her role as mom to five children. She truly seemed to be in charge.

One day in a class on parenting, Jackie spoke up: "It takes two to make an argument. Just make up your mind that you will not argue with the child. There will be no argument." Linda recalled a scene during one of her visits to Jackie's house at a time when she had four teenagers and one preteen. When her teenage son asked if he could go to the beach, Jackie just said, "No."

He kept begging, "Mom, can I go? Ple-e-e-ase!"

"I said no, and I will not change my mind," she responded. The youngster continued to bombard her with reasons why he should go swimming. Jackie heard him out. But she stuck to her quiet "no" position.

Linda decided to follow Jackie's practical, working example of how to be a mom who doesn't argue. When her own 11-year-old burst through the door after school one afternoon, he had big plans.

"Mom, can I go to Steven's house? We're going to clean out his hamster cage."

"No," Linda replied firmly. "Your room smells like a hamster cage. Go clean it up."

"But, Mom, I promised Steven I would be there," he complained.

Linda looked at him. She tried to show the same stern but loving authority she'd seen Jackie show her son. "No, Mark. Now go clean your room. I won't argue."

"Well, can I go after I clean my room?" Mark asked.

"Of course," Linda replied with a grin. It had worked. There had been no argument. She whispered a relieved, "Thank you, Lord." After he had cleaned his room and was about to run to his friend's house, Linda rewarded him with a pat on the shoulder. "Thanks, Mark," she said. "You did a great job. I'm proud of you."

Later Linda said, "If my children can learn at a young age to obey authority, they will be better suited to fit into God's family. Much of the chipping and training will be finished before they become adults."

Asserting authority as a parent goes with our job description. As much as we might want to be best friends or pals to our children, that facet of the relationship comes primarily after they become adults. During their formative years, we parents—with all our human frailties—are the most important authority figures in their lives. We must not abandon our responsibilities.

Struggles over Choices

When children approach their teen years, parents face the question of how much freedom to give them in choosing their friends, the kind of entertainment and music they watch and listen to, and where they will attend school.

When Pam and Gene clashed with their two daughters in these areas, they spent many hours praying for God's guidance. Finally they concluded that it was their responsibility to set the standards for their home. "Gene told them what type of movies and music would be allowed in our home, and both of us enforced these rules," Pam said.

During her eighth-grade year, Angie, the older daughter, and her two best friends were cheerleaders at a Christian school. When both friends decided to attend public school for their high school years, Pam and Gene felt God wanted their daughter to stay where she was. Angie tried every possible way to talk her parents into letting her leave, but they remained firm on the issue. Hard feelings and harsh words resulted, and they had a very unhappy teenager on their hands that summer.

But before school started again, the family attended a week-long conference about establishing a righteous family. Afterward her parents again told Angie they felt the Christian school was God's will for her. She now had a choice: she could go back to school in rebellion or go back willingly. She decided to do what her parents asked.

"As mothers, we often have to pray for God's direction and then obey, even when it is hard," Pam says. "But I've found that God always honors our obedience. In regard to dating, our two daughters agreed that they would bring all prospective dates to meet their dad and get his approval. For years we prayed our girls would marry only the man God chose for each of them. We believe God honored that because today we have two sons-in-law who love the Lord."

Love, Not Control

Moms have to choose their battles carefully. On some issues you must state what you will or will not allow and then not deviate from that position. But with other issues, you can be more flexible and allow your children to make choices for themselves, even when they differ from what you would choose. The important thing is always to respond with God's love. You never want to come across as a dictator.

Children need to know there are both privileges and consequences to living in a family. Abusing a privilege means living with the penalty. Protecting our children from the negative results of their wrong choices prevents them from learning responsibility. Some overly controlling parents are trapped into thinking they "own" their children. They make themselves both judge and jury with the idea, "I am the boss and what I say goes." Dr. Kevin Leman cautions that this approach is heavy into control and short on love and support. He writes:

> Our children belong to the Lord. He has given them to us 'on loan,' with specific guidelines in his Word for the training and enrichment of their lives. When we slip into the Super Parent Syndrome, we can try so hard and get so wrapped up in our children that we try to possess them...Reality discipline seeks to guide, not own or control...
>
> Parents are afraid to let their kids fail. I'm not saying that a child should be a failure by habit or that she should learn to be a loser in life. I am saying that we learn through failure...the home should be a place where failure is allowed. It is dealt with matter-of-factly and is cushioned with love and encouragement from the parents.[5]

Treating Children with Respect

Sandra was suddenly plunged into single parenthood when her husband lost his battle with cancer and she still had two young children to care for. She knew nothing about paying bills, budgeting, balancing a checkbook, doing home maintenance, or repairing a car. Yet she decided early on that, with God's help, they would survive as a family of three. She realized the only way her kids could develop their own strength was by watching her. So she would be careful to model Christian character.

Long before they reached their teens, Sandra talked to her kids about what she would expect of them. Twelve-year-old Holly and her mom even signed a "contract" about dating and other rules she agreed to observe.

When they were teenagers, friends were welcome to their home but none of them could drink, smoke, swear, or watch inappropriate movies while there. One night a group of kids went to a school hockey game and came to Sandra's afterward for pizza and a movie. The kids put their own movie in the video player, unaware that Sandra also had rented one.

When she passed through the family room after the movie started, Sandra knew immediately this was not a movie she wanted them to watch. She says in the midst of her "wimpy decision-making process" she heard a swear word on the program. That was it. She called Holly into the living room.

After they talked Sandra said, "Holly, you know the video is going to be turned off. Now would you like me to do that or would you rather take care of it yourself?"

"You are treating me like a baby," Holly complained.

"No, I'm treating you with the respect you deserve—exactly the way I expect your friends to treat me," Sandra replied. "If I thought you were a baby I would have thundered in there and turned it off myself. Out of respect for your maturity, I'm giving you the choice."

Holly chose to tell her friends herself. "Sorry, guys. My mom says we can't watch this." The boys quickly apologized.

During their teen years Sandra welcomed her children's friends—primarily because she wanted to keep tabs on what they were doing. "Peer pressure can be almost overwhelming at times, and to resist such pressure may take more strength than some teenagers can muster. At such times our kids need our support, not our rebuke," she says.

Sandra gave her children permission to use her as an excuse in intense pressure situations. They could just say, "I can't do that. My mom would kill me."[6]

While writing this book, I (Quin) asked Sandra how her children—adults now—are doing. "Both kids turned out great," she said. Then with a chuckle she added, "Contrary to what the media statistics would have us believe, neither of them ended up becoming an ax murderer!" We laughed together, grateful at what her perseverance and God's grace had accomplished.

Like Sandra, parents must decide how often their youngsters can watch TV and which programs are age-appropriate for them. Some moms and dads watch certain programs with their children and then discuss them afterward. One mom told her son, "God holds me responsible for what you watch in my home, and because I want what's best for you, I cannot let you watch what some of your friends are watching."

Rewards vs. Unconditional Love

As I (Quin) mentioned earlier, we used a "reward system" with our children during a certain period of their lives. At the time I didn't know any other family who did this, probably because we moms didn't discuss discipline problems. Discipline was considered a private matter!

Now, years later, I've read books such as *How to Really Love Your Child*, which explains how to use the "chart-with-stars" reward technique to help curb the fighting among siblings. One star was given for every 15 minutes of peace; then each boy received an appropriate reward for a certain number of stars. The author, Dr. Ross Campbell, says the system worked beautifully in his family.[7]

However, he warns against overuse of behavior modification as a substitute for emotional nurturing, emphasizing that we must guard against leading a child to behave in a certain way in order to get something he wants.[8]

"As you can tell, good child-rearing requires balance," he writes. "A child needs...eye contact, physical contact, focused attention, discipline, requests, firmness, flexibility, commands, forgiveness, punishment, behavior modification, instruction, guidance, example and active listening. But we must give our children these things in proper measure."[9]

May the Holy Spirit empower all of us to do these things in such a way that our children feel unconditionally loved.

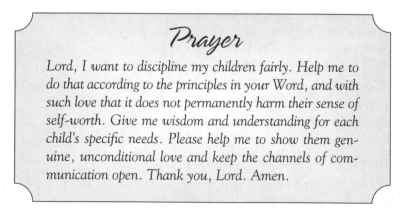

Prayer

Lord, I want to discipline my children fairly. Help me to do that according to the principles in your Word, and with such love that it does not permanently harm their sense of self-worth. Give me wisdom and understanding for each child's specific needs. Please help me to show them genuine, unconditional love and keep the channels of communication open. Thank you, Lord. Amen.

Scriptures for Meditation

"The fear of the LORD is the beginning of knowledge, but fools despise wisdom and discipline" (Proverbs 1:7).

"He who ignores discipline despises himself, but whoever heeds correction gains understanding" (Proverbs 15:32).

"Discipline your son, and he will give you peace; he will bring delight to your soul" (Proverbs 29:17).

"No discipline seems pleasant at the time, but painful. Later on, however, it produces a harvest of righteousness and peace for those who have been trained by it" (Hebrews 12:11).

"I keep my body under control and make it my slave, so I won't lose out after telling the good news to others" (1 Corinthians 9:27 CEV).

5
Power for Your "If Onlys"
Healing Your Guilt

"No one whose hope is in you will ever be put to shame...
Guard my life and rescue me; let me not be put to shame,
for I take refuge in you. May integrity and uprightness
protect me, because my hope is in you"
—PSALM 25:3, 20-21

There are two kinds of guilt most of us will struggle with:
true guilt (a result of our sin against God) and pseudo-guilt
(when there is no sin in our lives). When we have sinned, we must
confess it to God. The blood of Jesus takes care of true guilt by
doing two basic things: it washes away our sin—as though it never
had existed; it perfectly satisfies God's eternal justice.[1]
—R.T. KENDALL

ost of us moms, if we are honest, have suffered with "what if?" guilt. That voice in your head that says, "What if I had done this differently? What if I hadn't said that? What if I had paid more attention to the things my child said or did? Maybe I'm to blame for her rebellion..." And on and on it goes.

You may feel that if you hadn't made so many parenting mistakes, your children would be more likely to reach God's full potential for their lives. Or, even in cases where you have done the right thing by your kids, that it's simply too little too late.

As these "if only" scenarios play across your thoughts, you heap guilt on yourself. If you had prayed sooner, taught earlier, loved more, communicated better, perhaps such and such would not have happened.

The truth is that none of us is a perfect parent. Only Father God can claim that title. But because of his great love for us and for our children, God can redeem our mistakes when we cooperate with him. Though we can't change the past, we can ask the Holy Spirit to guide us and help us make amends as we move into the future with hope, not guilt.

I (Ruthanne) remember how plagued with guilt I was years ago when I forgot to pick up four-year-old Bradley from nursery school one day when it closed early, just before noon.

On that particular day my husband and I had an unusually busy program at the Bible school where we were teaching, and we simply forgot that it was Wednesday. When the director of the nursery school couldn't locate us at our home phone, she called our neighbor, whose child was also in Bradley's class. As soon as our neighbor saw our car stop in front of our house just after 2:00 P.M., she came out to tell us what had happened.

John jumped back in the car and took off for the school. By the time he arrived there the director had left, and he found Bradley sitting in the kitchen of the school housekeeper and eating a bowl of soup. This woman lived on the premises of the school, and because lunch wasn't served on the early-release day, she was kind enough to feed this hungry child whose parents had forgotten him.

Of course both my husband and I told Bradley how terribly sorry we were and promised him it would never happen again. But that didn't alleviate the self-reproach I felt—nor my embarrassment when we apologized to the school director the next day. For months afterward, Bradley was terrified to let me out of his sight when we were in a public place or when we dropped him off at school, his Sunday school class, or at a babysitter's home. I had to continually reassure him that Mommy and Daddy wouldn't forget to come back for him, and in time his fear diminished.

Don't Dwell on Your Failure

Guilt is the air moms breathe. Whether struggling with everyday guilt for not being able to "do it all" or retrospective guilt for our mistakes as a parent, dealing with this powerful emotion is a mom's fact of life. The truth is, we can drown in a sea of "what ifs" if we allow guilt and shame to consume us. Because we often confuse these two emotions, let's examine their meanings.

Guilt is the sense of regret we feel about something we did—our behavior. When we feel guilty, we are taking on the blame for some committed offense, even if we didn't realize at the time how damaging the end results could be. Then there is *false guilt*, what we feel when we take on the blame for a situation over which we had no control.

Shame, on the other hand, relates to how we feel about ourselves—our self image. Meanings of shame include disgrace, dishonor, humiliation, and reproach. If we don't receive God's forgiveness to erase our guilt, the added burden of shame can turn us inward until we convince ourselves, "I'm just not a very good mom."

We want to encourage you to acknowledge your real mistakes, to seek the Lord's forgiveness, to pray for power against false guilt, and to lay hold of the grace that God offers each of us when our conduct is less than perfect. In some cases you may need to ask your child to forgive you. When done with true humility, such an action can go a long way to restoring the breach and mending the relationship.

But once you have received God's forgiveness, you must also forgive yourself if you are truly to be free from guilt and shame. Pastor Kendall explains why this is so important:

> If I let myself dwell on my failure, I am giving in to
> pseudo-guilt and sinning as I do because I am digni-
> fying unbelief…The bottom line is this: Not forgiving
> ourselves is wrong and dishonoring to God. But God
> will use the sorrow we feel over what we've done to
> draw us to Himself.[2]

Here's a powerful antidote for guilt: "Let us draw near to God
with a sincere heart in full assurance of faith, having our hearts
sprinkled to cleanse us from a guilty conscience" (Hebrews
10:22).

Are You Being Fair?

Once I (Quin) was talking to Jodie, a Christian nurse tending
to my husband in the hospital. She confided to me she was so
upset with her third-grader for bringing home a low math grade
on her report card that she had decided not to give her a party
the following weekend for her eighth birthday.

"Is that really fair?" I asked. "Think how bad you will feel later
on when your daughter has only painful memories of her eighth
birthday because Mom cancelled her party. Isn't there some other
way you can work with her to improve her math grade?"

Jodie looked surprised. "I never thought of it as wounding
her," she said. "It just made me angry because I know she can do
better, and I'm trying to get her to be more serious about her
school work."

"Maybe you need to forgive her for disappointing you and tell
her so," I urged. "You can ask God to show you another way to
deal with the math problem, and I believe he will."

"I'll think about it," she promised.

The next day Jodie came into the hospital room smiling.

"I told my daughter I was sorry for getting angry, and that I
forgive her for not making higher marks in math," she said. "I'm
going to help her with some extra study time to deal with the

math problem. She's so excited about the party—she's making her list of friends to invite."

"Good going, Mom," I said, giving her a thumbs-up. "Now you won't have to deal with a load of guilt, and I'm sure you're going to have a great party that she will always remember."

Another mom confessed to me one time that she struggled with shame because she strongly disliked her youngest child, five-year-old Candy. "I yell at her more than the others. It seems she's always the one who starts trouble when there's a squabble among the three kids," she said. "It's just impossible for me to love her unconditionally."

When I probed a bit deeper about this mom's situation, I learned that while she was pregnant with Candy, her husband had left her for a younger woman. She admitted she had allowed her anger toward him to transfer to their daughter, causing her to unconsciously blame this innocent child for the breakup of the marriage. And it was clear that her guilt and shame were only compounding the problem.

With a repentant heart she prayed, "Lord, I forgive my daughter. I forgive my husband. Please forgive me and take away my shame." Later she wrote and told me her whole attitude had changed, and that she now had a new love for her little girl.

If you are a mom of young children, you've probably had some skirmishes with guilt already. But as one experienced mom observed, "When your kids become teenagers, then you *really* find out how powerful guilt can be!" The example in our next story may be helpful as your children grow older and you deal with conflicts that often arise with teenagers.

With Love, Forgiveness Comes

Nancy is a mom who struggled with her emotions when her 16-year-old, Rhonda, ran away from home for three days. Upon her return she showed no remorse for the emotional roller-coaster ride she had put her parents through. *I should be glad she's home, but she doesn't act as if she's done anything wrong*, Nancy fumed silently. She knew she needed to forgive Rhonda, but her anger and guilt were in the way.

As hard as it was to do, Nancy found that being brutally honest with the Lord about her feelings helped her to get back on track. In church a few days after her daughter's return, Nancy talked to God about her hurts.

"I don't even like Rhonda. She's not pleasant to be around, and the house is always in turmoil when she's home," she lamented in her prayer. "Frankly, I don't think she even cares she put us through so much anxiety by running away. Lord, how can I love her, let alone forgive her?"

The Holy Spirit's response was almost immediate. After her honest prayer, the Lord seemed to turn back the clock in Nancy's mind. She pictured little Rhonda standing on a chair with an apron tied around her waist, waiting to help her mom dry dishes. Then she saw a flash of her bundled up with coat and mittens on a winter day, standing in the snow beside the laundry basket, handing Mom her brother's diapers to hang. She had been so lovable then.

Then in her thoughts Nancy saw Rhonda in second grade, bringing home a valentine with her picture on it that showed her grin with a missing front tooth. As the memories paraded through her mind, and she remembered how much she had loved this child, Nancy's heart softened.

"Lord, restore that love to me, because with that love, I know forgiveness will come," she prayed. In a moment, God sovereignly flooded Nancy's heart with a deep love for Rhonda—almost more than she could contain.

"Not only did I love her, I even liked her again!" Nancy exclaimed. "I forgave her for hurting me and asked God to forgive me for my wrong attitude."

Though the teenager continued to cause her mom anxiety throughout her high school years, Nancy had won the victory over her feelings. "From the day God renewed my love for Rhonda, I was able to respond to her with genuine love and forgiveness," she said.

Somewhere along the way, that love melted Rhonda's heart. During one visit home after she had gone away to college, she mentioned some of the daredevil things she'd done in earlier years. "I never said I was sorry, Mom. Please forgive me for all I put you through," she begged.

The forgiveness had come full circle.[3]

Rhonda is now trusting God to help her become a Spirit-led single mom to her own newly adopted daughter. The responsibility of becoming a parent has motivated this once troublesome child to draw closer to the Lord than she's ever been, much to Nancy's delight.

Perhaps you are going through a situation with your children and being assailed by anger and guilt. You can call on God exactly as Nancy did. He responds to our sincere cries for his help with love and assurance, just as we do when one of our children sincerely appeals for our help. The Holy Spirit can give you creative ideas for expressing love to a difficult child, or help you discover an unlikely solution for a thorny problem.

Looking at Guilt Realistically

Every mom who contends with feeling guilty when her child makes a wrong choice needs to realize this: Many factors outside her control influence her children and contribute to their decisions. These considerations don't absolve the child's responsibility—they simply help put the problem in perspective. A guilt-laden mom's energy can best be spent praying for her child and asking the Holy Spirit to show her how to reach that one with love and acceptance.

Because God created us with free will, each of us has the freedom to make choices. When we make wrong choices, we must live with the consequences. Learning this truth is central to reaching responsible adulthood, and as moms, we need the Holy Spirit's help to convey this reality to our children. At the same time, we must assure them that our love for them is unconditional. We love them even when they make wrong choices because that's the way God loves us.

"Give your children unconditional love no matter how much they embarrass you or go against what you have taught them," one mom wrote us. "Let them know they are loved without any strings attached."

Forgiveness and Love Go Hand in Hand

Attacking a mom's mind with guilt—whether real or false— often seems to be the enemy's weapon of choice. But for a mom who has a strained relationship with her stepchild or an adopted child, the struggle is especially difficult.

Recently I (Ruthanne) met a mom with three young sons— I'll call her Yvonne—who was suffering over the guilt she felt because of her anger toward her stepdaughter. I had just taught a session about breaking free from the bondage of unforgiveness, and afterward she came to me for counsel and prayer.

"I knew my husband had fathered a child out of wedlock before we were married," she said. "He had repented for his sin and received God's forgiveness, and the child's mother said she didn't want him to have any involvement with the girl. So we determined to go on with our lives. But when she was 12 years old, the girl told her mom she wanted to live with her father, and my husband felt we had to receive her. I had a very hard time accepting her."

Yvonne's tears flowed freely as she shared how she had struggled to show love to young Patty, who, up until this time, apparently had lived in a very undisciplined and ungodly household. Yvonne's primary concern was to prevent her from being a negative influence on her sons. After many months filled with quarrels and conflict, Patty ran away to a relative's house.

"My husband is so angry he wants nothing to do with her now," she said. "I feel the whole problem is partly my fault because I didn't accept her and love her when she was in my home. Now she's about to become a teenager, and I'm afraid of what might happen to her because she's out of control."

I helped Yvonne to see that, through no fault of her own, Patty was a victim of the corrupt environment she had grown up in, and that Yvonne and her husband could be instrumental in turning the child's life around. After all, they are the only people in Patty's life who know the Lord and can be a godly example to her. As Yvonne wept, I led her in a prayer in which she told the Lord that she forgave Patty, and she asked forgiveness for her own wrong attitudes and actions. Then we prayed together that God would reveal his love to Patty and bring her to salvation.

"When you go home, tell your husband that you have forgiven Patty and prayed for her," I told Yvonne. "Then urge him to do the same, and let Patty know that both of you have chosen to forgive her. If you and your husband begin praying in agreement for her—and then reach out to her in love as the Lord leads—I believe, over time, you will see the situation change." I concluded by suggesting that she ask the Lord to give them creative ideas for acknowledging Patty's birthday with a gift that would be a concrete expression of their love and concern.

I am hoping to hear from Yvonne again someday with a good report of how God is working in their family.

Peace Can Replace Guilt

Moms who feel overcome with guilt when a child strays from his Christian roots can use their energy in a productive way by asking the Holy Spirit for guidance as to how to pray effectively for the prodigal. Wallowing in remorse does nothing to change the situation. The good news is that rebels with a strong Christian background often return to their faith at some point in life.

Dr. James Dobson, founder of Focus on the Family, conducted a survey of 35,000 parents regarding their children's acceptance of the Christian values with which they had been raised. He reports:

> As can be observed, 53 percent of even the most strong-willed and rebellious children eventually return to the values of their parents, outright. When that figure is combined with those who are "somewhat" accepting of parental perspectives, that means 85 percent of those hardheaded, independent individuals will eventually lean toward their parents' point of view by the time adolescence is over. Only 15 percent are so headstrong that they reject everything their family stood for, and I'll wager that there were other problems and sources of pain in most of these cases.
>
> What this means, in effect, is that these tough-minded kids will fuss and fight and complain throughout their years at home, but the majority will turn around as young adults and do what their parents most desired…If we could evaluate these individuals at 35 instead of 24 years of age, even fewer would still be in rebellion against parental values.[4]

I (Quin) once encountered a mother at a conference who was weighed down with guilt because she harbored resentment against her only son. Refusing to let go of anything wrong he had ever done, she rehearsed unhappy incidents over and over in her mind. Obviously, the woman was miserable. I talked to her about her need to forgive and accept him and suggested she could use each new day as an opportunity to repair the breach with her son.

"I have taught him the Bible, and we have family devotions," she said. "I've done everything I can to raise him to do right, but he keeps disappointing me by doing dumb, outlandish things that embarrass me. Then I feel guilty about being ashamed of him."

"What's passed is in the past—it's history," I told her. "Start today to build a new relationship with him. Why not write him a card or letter and let him know how much you appreciate some of his good qualities? Surely he has some if you would just forgive him, cast off your guilt, and look for the positives in him. You may be surprised at how such an act of kindness on your part may affect him—if not now, later on in life."

She hung her head and said she would think about it, but at that moment it was just too difficult. I walked away wondering if she truly realized what toxic baggage she was carrying in her heart.

An Amazing Gift of Hope

Guilt often comes with the added weight of regret. When our children fall into pits of their own choosing, we moms struggle with agonizing feelings of "what might have been." This is particularly true if a son or daughter who has made wrong choices dies prematurely.

When Freda's 21-year-old son, Michael, was killed instantly in a car crash, she was tempted to say, "Surely there's something I could have done to prevent this." She had invested many hours in praying for Michael because of his recurring problems with drug addiction. She didn't even know for sure whether he was on the road to recovery when the accident took his life.

Then one day she received a package of Michael's belongings from the wrecked car. Inside were a journal and letters he had written to each of his parents acknowledging his Christian upbringing and expressing his honor and love for them. What an amazing gift of hope this was to her.

Freda's guilt was lifted when she read these words from her son: "I want you to know that I couldn't have hoped for a mama who cared more about me. I also want you to know that I don't blame you at all for the way I turned out. It's not your fault. I love you."

But the letter Freda treasures most was this:

Dear Mama,

I want to apologize for that time when you wouldn't let me do what I wanted, and I told you that I had never felt any love coming from you. That was intended to hurt you, and it was an evil thing to do. I still hear you crying sometimes. It's the most awful sound I've ever heard. I could hear it through the wall plainly, and it seemed to last forever. I was so ashamed, and I wanted to come and hug you and tell you that I didn't mean it. But I didn't, and I am so sorry. I hope you believe that I would erase it if I could, because I would.

I can look back now and see that you do love me, more than I understand, and that you always have. I couldn't have hoped for a mom who cared more about me.

I love you.

—Michael

"Everybody has different experiences, but I believe everyone's choices bring consequences," Freda says when she speaks to school and church groups. She points out that Michael's aspiration was to become an English teacher, but his addiction took all that away. "If I can help just one person—keep one kid from drugs—it's worth my pain to share about Michael," she said. God's peace has replaced her guilt, and the "if onlys" no longer plague her.

Make Your Decision

Maybe right now you want to release your "if onlys" to God, get rid of prolonged guilt, and move on to a higher level of trust in your heavenly Father. If you have asked God to forgive you, then *accept* his forgiveness. Countless women we have met tell us they don't *feel* forgiven, even though they've repented and asked for God's forgiveness over and over for the same sin.

We encourage them—and you—to speak aloud and make a declaration to the enemy:

> I have confessed my sin, and according to God's promise in 1 John 1:9, I am forgiven. Because I accept his forgiveness, guilt must go, in Jesus' name!

This can be your step to walking out of guilt once and for all. You no longer need to punish yourself for your mistakes.

Prayer

Lord, thank you that Jesus went to the cross to pay for my sin. Thank you that I can come to you with my guilty conscience and have it cleansed. I receive your forgiveness. Thank you that every day I can start anew, trusting you to see me through whatever struggle I am facing. Lord, I thank you for wiping away my guilt and letting me see you with new eyes. Thank you, too, for loving and forgiving my children. Please send your Holy Spirit to minister your love to them, even as you are renewing and restoring me. I love you, Lord. Amen.

Scriptures for Meditation

"He does not treat us as our sins deserve or repay us according to our iniquities. For as high as the heavens are above the earth, so great is his love for those who fear him; as far as the east is from the west, so far has he removed our transgressions from us" (Psalm 103:10-12).

"He was wounded for our transgressions, He was bruised for our guilt and iniquities; the chastisement [needful to obtain] peace and well-being for us was upon Him, and with the stripes [that wounded] Him we are healed and made whole" (Isaiah 53:5 AMP).

"Then you will know the truth, and the truth will set you free...So if the Son sets you free, you will be free indeed" (John 8:32,36).

"Therefore, if anyone is in Christ, he is a new creation; the old has gone, the new has come!" (2 Corinthians 5:17).

"If we confess our sins, he is faithful and just and will forgive us our sins and purify us from all unrighteousness" (1 John 1:9).

6

Power to Find Answers

Seeking God's Wisdom and Discernment

*But the wisdom that comes from heaven is first of all pure;
then peace-loving, considerate, submissive, full of mercy
and good fruit, impartial and sincere. Peacemakers who
sow in peace raise a harvest of righteousness.*
—JAMES 3:17-18

*As long as we think we can handle it all, we will.
Unless we grasp what we can't do, we won't have
a clue to what God can do.*[1]
—ELISA MORGAN

oday's mom needs the Holy Spirit's discernment to understand each of her children and to help her apply scriptural wisdom to the tough questions of mothering. Discernment includes recognizing God's voice and then obeying what he tells you to do. A Spirit-led mom will choose to follow his voice, even if doing so runs counter to conventional wisdom. Walking closely with the Lord is important, for when we keep an attitude of openness to his leading, his voice may come unexpectedly, as the following stories illustrate.

To Homeschool or Not?

As today's young moms face difficult decisions about their children's education, many of them are praying about whether to send their children to school (public or private) or to home-school them. Because these choices will have lifelong effects, they need the help of the Holy Spirit as they carefully weigh all the options. We were surprised to discover that the number of children in the U.S. who are homeschooled is now estimated at two million, and the trend is growing at about 15 percent per year.[2]

I (Ruthanne) recently visited our younger daughter, Melody, and asked her how she reached the decision to teach her three children at home.

"Homeschooling is something I never ever wanted to do, and I didn't see why it would be necessary for my kids," she said. "We live in an area that reportedly has good schools, so I enrolled Rachel in public school kindergarten. Wanting to be an involved parent, I volunteered as a teacher's helper on the one morning a week my two younger ones were in a 'mom's day out' program. But it didn't take long for me to become disillusioned with the public education system."

Helping out in her daughter's classroom, Melody was dismayed to see that more than half of the time Rachel was in class was spent either standing in line for one thing or another, or waiting while the teacher checked the roll, tried to get the class quiet, or dealt with discipline issues. Then, about five months into the school year, the teacher began repeating the same curriculum all over again. Rachel, along with several others in the class of 22, was becoming bored and listless.

Melody discreetly mentioned to the teacher that a lot of the children seemed just on the verge of being able to read. "Why can't they keep going forward, instead of repeating material they've already learned?" she asked.

"Oh, we have to repeat the curriculum to be sure the slower ones are ready for first grade," the teacher said. "They'll learn to read next year."

Melody was well aware that some members of the class were struggling through no fault of their own. Part of her assignment was to sit behind the kids when they formed their reading circles and jostle awake the ones who fell asleep while the teacher was reading to them.

"It made me really upset with parents who send their children to school without sufficient food and sleep, making it hard for them to learn," she said. "I felt sorry for these kids, but I didn't think it was fair to keep my child in this school environment where she was being held back for the sake of the slower ones. Then I learned that Rachel had a special problem with her hearing that made it difficult for her to block out background noises and focus on what the teacher was saying in class. When she was scolded for not following instructions—because she hadn't properly understood them—she became upset and withdrawn."

Fearing her child would not get the attention she needed in this public school, Melody explored the possibility of private schools in the area. But she quickly realized that even if she went back to work, she wouldn't be able to earn enough to pay Rachel's tuition, plus childcare for the two younger ones, and, later on, tuition for all three. About this time one of her friends asked whether she had considered homeschooling.

"Oh, I can't do that," she replied. But the friend told her about a national homeschoolers convention coming up that was being held in their city, and she urged Melody to at least go check it out. "I went, feeling very doubtful that I could actually homeschool Rachel," Melody said. "But when I walked into the huge exhibit hall I realized two things: A lot of other people had the same problem I did, and there was plenty of help available.

Because other doors were closing, I felt I should at least try this option for a while."

She ordered supplies and started Rachel in first grade in July—so that just in case the experiment didn't work, she would still have time to enroll her in public school in August. Melody's homeschooling was a huge success. By October Rachel was able to read second- to third-grade level material. And to this mom's great surprise, four-year-old Lydia began listening in on the lessons. By the time she started kindergarten she had an advanced vocabulary and already understood some math principles. Soon the youngest, Joel, also was one of her pupils, and she's now completing her eighth year of homeschooling.

"I am not a militant homeschooler who feels that sending your kids to public school is like sending them to the devil," Melody said. "But I feel this is the option God led me to pursue to do what is best for our children, and my husband supports my position, even though he's not able to help with the teaching. Now that Rachel is ready for high school, I'm aware that I may have to do considerably more learning alongside her—but then, I've never had all the answers anyway.

"Life is as much a learning process for the homeschool mom as for the students! But God is faithful, and he seems to drop in my lap the curriculum that works best for us, and I can get help through homeschool co-ops for the more difficult subjects. Going through this process, I wasn't consciously aware that the Holy Spirit was leading me to homeschool, but now I realize that was the case."

An added bonus, Melody has discovered, is that she can be flexible with their school hours to accommodate the kids' busy schedule of private music lessons, and Rachel's and Lydia's participation in a youth orchestra.

She Chose Public School

Cynthia is a part-time working mom of two who says that because of her husband's help, she is able to work outside the home and still be involved in her children's schooling experiences. Steve vacuums the house, mows the lawn, and takes out the garbage. Before going to his own job, he drives ten-year-old Shawn and seven-year-old Lana to school by 7:30 every morning, where they have extracurricular sports activities before classes begin.

"One of the most important decisions Steve and I ever made was to put our children in public school," Cynthia reports. "We had to hear from God on this—not other people—and do what we thought was best for our children. We have friends and relatives who are either homeschooling or have enrolled their children in Christian schools, and they offered advice. But we had a conviction and we stuck to it. It has turned out that our ministry outreach is at our children's school, where we are very involved. I volunteer in Shawn's and Lana's classrooms two hours a week, and I'm active in the fundraising carnival which brings in as much as $15,000 for our school each year."

Cynthia feels a sense of peace when her home is tidy, but if she learns that on her day off one of her kids is having a field trip, she goes with them as a chaperone instead of cleaning house. That's because she takes seriously her responsibility of being a school volunteer.

"Since I started working at our church three years ago, I've lowered my expectations about my house," she said with a laugh. "Fast is good; simple is fine. If I can get a quick dish on the table for supper without intense labor these days, that's what I do."

During the summer Steve works four ten-hour days while she adjusts her part-time schedule to one and a half full days. That way they are available as much as possible to be with the children. "I do sympathize with single working moms who don't have the support from a husband like I do," she says. "And I'm blessed with good kids who don't give me heavy discipline problems."

Her job at their church keeps her on her toes spiritually as she oversees more than 40 Sunday school teachers. But Cynthia doesn't berate herself if she occasionally misses her Bible reading time.

"I have experienced God's grace and mercy, and I know he still loves me even if I am too busy to read on a particular day," she says. "I do find that nights are my best time to pray."

We asked Cynthia what advice she might give to other mothers seeking to walk closer to the Lord.

"Listen to God and do what he wants you to do. The quicker you learn to hear and obey his voice, the sooner you will know peace. Also, take time for yourself—you will be a better mom as a result."

Making decisions about a child's schooling is difficult in the best of circumstances. But for a mom with a special needs child, the problem becomes even more complicated, as our friend Ann discovered.

Sometimes Mom Has to Be a Drill Sergeant

"I think we are often led by the Holy Spirit when we don't realize it—even when we're not consciously seeking guidance," Ann told us recently.

She is a single mom whose adopted daughter, Luci, age four-and-a-half, suffers from cerebral palsy, which, in her case, resulted in a significant speech delay—a condition called *apraxia*. Luci can understand what people say to her but has great difficulty responding. Realizing she needed to be proactive to ensure that her child would learn how to speak, Ann tried everything she could that might help.

"It was frustrating to know how to help her," Ann said. "Luci attended a special education preschool, and we spent six weeks one summer in an out-of-town speech therapy program, but her progress still seemed slow. Though Luci is bright, I worried she might never be able to attend a regular school because no one would be able to understand her. I knew, too, that Luci could be resistant to speech therapy. Like most of us, Luci doesn't like doing what doesn't come naturally. And that made it tough for me to keep practicing her therapy at home because it doesn't come naturally for me to keep pushing her. I just wanted her to develop normally as my other daughter had done."

One evening, when Ann was feeling particularly discouraged, she logged onto her e-mail and read a posting from a newsgroup for parents of children with this condition. One of the moms in the group told the story of the amazing progress her daughter was making. She described herself as a "drill sergeant," refusing to allow her child to quit working on her speech no matter what.

"Her words hit me, and I thought, *That's what Luci needs*," Ann said. "Though I hated the idea of becoming a drill sergeant to my child, I resolved then and there that if that mom could do it, I could do it. For Luci's sake, I couldn't give up.

"But what struck me even more strongly about this woman's posting was the verse from Scripture she closed with: 'And let us not be weary in well doing: for in due season we shall reap, if we faint not (Galatians 6:9 KJV).' I decided that was a pretty good motto for any mother, so I adopted it as my own. No more fainting in my spirit when things got tough. No more giving into discouragement. No more internal complaining. Now, when I am tempted to give up, I look at that verse I pasted onto my computer. It seems like a promise God has made to me personally: I will reap a reward on behalf of my child if I keep at it."

Ann determined to stick with the therapy routines and to be more diligent in helping Luci verbally respond to messages, even when she wanted to use other ways to communicate. Since then, Luci has made continued progress—so much so that her preschool teachers expressed their amazement when she returned after summer break. Now, instead of resisting therapy, Luci is working hard to learn to speak on her own. She still has a ways to go, but her progress is encouraging to everyone, most especially to her.

Ann is grateful that God's Spirit spoke to her through an unexpected source—the words and experience of another mom who would not allow herself to "be weary in well doing" on behalf of her child. It was the right word at the right time, a word that keeps on strengthening her for the trials and struggles ahead.

Knowing When to Let Go

Parenting is filled with questions. Which friends provide the most positive influence? Which activities are appropriate for each child? Which training program or college is best? When should a parent intervene, versus allowing the child to take risks and face the consequences?

I (Ruthanne) have often prayed Isaiah 54:13 for my children. The verse says, "All your children shall be taught by the LORD, and great shall be the peace of your children" (NKJV). One day while praying for my son, I paraphrased the verse something like this: "My son shall be taught of the Lord, and great shall be his peace."

Suddenly I was aware of God's still, small voice speaking to my heart: *If you want me to be his teacher, then you must get out of the way.*

My response was to explain to God that this headstrong 17-year-old was on a collision course with a brick wall. Because of a bad report from his teacher, I had scheduled an appointment for a tutor to coach Bradley for his final algebra exam. Claiming the problems were his teacher's fault, he had declared angrily that he wouldn't go to a tutor. We were in a stand-off on the matter.

Maybe hitting a brick wall is the only way he will learn, the Holy Spirit whispered. *After all, how did you learn your lessons?*

It's true for most of us that we learn best by hard experience. I agonized over the consequences my son would face later if he failed algebra, but I obeyed the Lord and canceled the appointment. I discovered how painful it is to truly commit your child into God's hands.

Sure enough, Bradley failed his final exam in algebra. He managed to pass the course with the lowest grade he had ever received in any class, but he lost his membership in the National Honor Society. That was bad enough, but only the following year did we learn the greater consequence.

He had applied to a top university for admission and a scholarship. After passing several levels of the acceptance process, he was in the pool of candidates for the few slots open in the school of architecture. But in the final cut he didn't make it. I was sure it was because of his low grade in algebra.

The day he came home and found his rejection letter, he stormed upstairs in a fit of anger and disappointment. "Oh, Lord," I prayed, "I know he must learn this lesson, but it's so painful to see him devastated like this."

Through my tears the Lord spoke to me very gently: *Don't worry, I won't hurt him anymore than I have to. He was mine before he was yours, and I love him more than you do.*

God was gracious to open another opportunity for Bradley to study architecture, and has faithfully continued to be my son's teacher. But for me, that experience was the beginning of a "letting go" process that has continued through the years.

Discerning the Voice of the Holy Spirit

The two previous stories, each involving a problem with a child wanting to do things in his or her own way, are an interesting contrast. Both Quin and I feel that when children are young, we moms should intervene as necessary to be sure our kids are properly nourished, trained, educated, disciplined, and so on. And that is exactly what the Lord led Ann to do for Luci.

But as they grow older, children gradually make more and more decisions on their own, learning along the way that they then must live with the results of those choices. At some point in your own child's development, you probably will sense the Holy Spirit speaking to you about "letting go" in a particular area.

Please don't hesitate to follow his leading and trust God for the outcome.

Each child and each situation is different, though. So how do we know when to step in and when to step back? Based on human reasoning alone, it's difficult to know. That is why we need the guidance of the Holy Spirit.

And this leads to yet another question. How can I know whether it truly is the Holy Spirit speaking to me? There are three possibilities to consider:

1. *The Holy Spirit can speak to you* by many different means. The most common ways are through Scripture, a sermon, a Bible lesson, a song you hear, an incident or phenomenon of nature you observe, a word given through another believer, or a still, small voice speaking to your mind. In all of these things, keep in mind that the Holy Spirit will always speak in a manner consistent with Scripture and with God's character.

2. *The enemy can speak to your mind*—and sometimes what you hear may at first seem to be perfectly logical. But if the message brings condemnation, guilt, depression, hopelessness, fear, or negative, destructive thoughts, you know that is not consistent with God's character. When you realize that the enemy is speaking, you should resist him and command him to be silent (see 1 Peter 5:8-9).

3. *Your own inner voice* may be the source of what you "hear" in your mind. This message will be based on your own will, your human reasoning, or your self-centered emotions.

When you are seeking the Lord for specific guidance about a matter, and you want to be sure you respond to the right voice, we suggest you pray a prayer something like this:

Lord, I come to you asking for guidance about this situation:_____(state the problem)_____. I refuse to hear the voice of the enemy or to be swayed by the voice of my own human desires or reasoning. Lord, my heart is open to hear only your voice. Please speak to me and reveal any action you want me to take, and show me when I should take it. Thank you that I can trust you to be the way, the truth, and the light for me. Amen.

God Promises His Wisdom

Sometimes moms have to take the role of a judge when trying to settle disputes between siblings. And during their years in school, moms must keep their spiritual ears alert as to the kind of teachings their kids are exposed to.

A Spirit-led mom may occasionally find herself taking an unpopular stand on issues that administrators and other parents seem unconcerned about. Yet, with the Bible as her standard, she should hold fast to truth. Her children's minds and spirits are at risk!

When Rae learned that books on magic and sorcery were being read aloud at the Christian school her two children attended, she was greatly disturbed. At the time, movies about a 10-year-old orphan boy were box office sellouts. The central figure in the series becomes a powerful wizard by taking classes to learn such things as casting spells, creating potions, and engaging in other occult practices. Students were being introduced to this "hero" through books about his adventures—books which could easily spark a child's interest in occult activity.

Deeply concerned, Rae determined to take action. But first she prayed for wisdom about how to respond and did research on the topic. She learned that these children's books had been challenged more than 400 times in schools in at least 20 states.

Inquiring at four other local Christian schools about their policies, she learned that all of them had banned the books. Even some of the public schools she called forbade their use.

Next, she agreed with two other parents to raise the issue with members of their school board. What really surprised her was that only three other parents were concerned enough to participate in this meeting. In the meantime, Rae printed out several pages of Scriptures which forbid witchcraft and made copies to give to the board members—including these:

> There shall not be found among you anyone who makes his son or his daughter pass through the fire, or one who practices witchcraft, or a soothsayer, or one who interprets omens, or a sorcerer, or one who conjures spells, or a medium, or a spiritist, or one who calls up the dead. For all who do these things are an abomination to the LORD (Deuteronomy 18:10-12 NKJV).

> Many also of those who had believed kept coming, confessing and disclosing their practices. And many of those who practiced magic brought their books together and began burning them in the sight of everyone (Acts 19:18-19 NASB).

Not long after the board meeting, Rae received a letter from the principal stating that teachers now could not read the books for their classes, but the books were to remain in the library for children to check out with a written note from a parent. The following year Rae decided not to reenroll her children in that school.

Cleanse Your Home

A Spirit-led mom watches carefully all that goes on in her household and is alert to the enemy's attempt to infiltrate her home. There are two sources of power in our world: that which comes from God and his kingdom and that which comes from Satan's kingdom. In New Testament times the world was full of superstition, magic, and idolatry. It remains so today.

We suggest that you do a thorough "spiritual housecleaning" of your home. Pray for the Holy Spirit's leading as you evaluate videos, computer games, music cassettes or CDs, trading cards, books, magazines, board games, posters, T-shirts, pictures, ceremonial articles or clothing, statues, and jewelry. The Holy Spirit can guide you about removing any items which compromise the Christian atmosphere you desire to maintain in your home.

Some ways you can help to safeguard your home include:

- Dedicate your home to the Lord and invite his presence to abide there.

- Pray over your family members at night and ask for their health and safety, even if you do it after they sleep.

- Ask the Holy Spirit to reveal to you anything objectionable in your house. You can go from room to room asking, "Is Jesus pleased with this room and everything in it?"

Unity Brings Peace

Maria is extremely protective of her children because she herself was once involved in the occult and she knows how unscriptural and damaging it is. Because of this, she has made decisions not all parents will be led to make, but they are right for her home. She doesn't want her children playing games, reading books, or watching cartoons with occultic images or themes.

At first her husband didn't see much wrong with allowing their children to watch such cartoons. Maria prayed, "Lord, please show my husband why this is wrong. Open his eyes. Help me to uphold what your Word says about not bringing a detestable thing—the images of other gods—into our home. Protect my children's minds and spirits."

When their oldest son entered first grade, he began showing an unhealthy interest in cards that had pictures of various little demons on them. He said the kids at school traded them. Maria firmly forbade him to have the cards and explained why from the Bible. One day when she was walking out of a store with her three children, a security guard stopped her. Her seven-year-old son had stolen a pack of the cards and hidden them in his pocket.

This was an eye-opener for her husband, and he began reading information about how occult groups use various devices to draw kids into a deceptive web. Cute games, he decided, could be harmful, so he reinforced Maria's position on the matter.

"I noticed a complete change in our home's atmosphere when he stood with me in opposing certain things in our house," Maria told us. "Not only did we have a sense of peace in our home, but our kids knew we were in unity about our decisions."

Helen and Tim are another couple who have agreed they will guard the Christian atmosphere in their home, and they enforce boundaries for their five- and eight-year-old.

"We preview videos before we let our kids watch them," Helen said. "And we spend a lot of family time together biking or playing board games. I also read to the children a lot. They have had gym and swimming lessons, and they play with friends they meet through church or their Christian school. It's important for me to make sure I get up ahead of the family to spend quality time with the Lord every morning to get his help for raising my children."

The road to adulthood in today's culture requires a parent to cope with more options and greater pressure than at any time in history. We also live in an era when parents have more helps and "how-to's" available to them than at any other time. However, because each child walking this road is God's unique creation, we moms also need the Holy Spirit's wisdom and discernment in making right choices. This help and insight can only be found in relying on the Holy Spirit's guidance.

Prayer

Lord, please give me great discernment for the day-to-day decisions I must make in raising my children in a way that honors you. I don't want my decisions to be based on the world's value system or on my own ideas or emotions, but on godly principles. Lord, teach me to hear the voice of the Holy Spirit, and help me to have a heart willing to obey his guidance. Thank you for answering my prayer. Amen.

Scriptures for Meditation

"I will instruct you and teach you in the way you should go; I will counsel you and watch over you" (Psalm 32:8).

"Teach me, O LORD, to follow your decrees; then I will keep them to the end. Give me understanding, and I will keep your law and obey it with all my heart. Direct me in the path of your commands, for there I find delight" (Psalm 119:33-35).

"Get wisdom, get understanding; do not forget my words or swerve from them" (Proverbs 4:5).

"Whether you turn to the right or to the left, your ears will hear a voice behind you, saying, 'This is the way; walk in it'" (Isaiah 30:21).

"I keep asking that the God of our Lord Jesus Christ, the glorious Father, may give you the Spirit of wisdom and revelation, so that you may know him better" (Ephesians 1:17).

"If any of you lacks wisdom, he should ask God, who gives generously to all without finding fault, and it will be given to him" (James 1:5).

7

Power to Forgive

Giving and Receiving Grace

When you stand praying, if you hold anything against anyone,
forgive him, so that your Father in heaven
may forgive you your sins.
—MARK 11:25

Sometimes I tell people to take all this hurt, put it in their hands,
hold their hands up to God, and give it all to Him.
He is the only one who can give peace. He is the only one
who can bring our children through to their God-given potential.
They may not be meeting our expectations and dreams,
but God can fulfill His will in their lives if we let Him.
As parents, it is important for us to allow Him to guide
our children and work in them without blocking Him
with our anger, bitterness, and sorrow.[1]
—JOYCE THOMPSON

All children need the assurance of Mom's forgiveness when they do something wrong. Parents need forgiving too. Sometimes what we really need is the humility to request and receive forgiveness from our family members—even our children—for our mistakes.

In this chapter we will examine biblical principles of forgiveness and also share stories from moms who have learned to apply them to their own lives. You will be encouraged by their experiences, and perhaps even recognize your own struggles in these examples.

How One Mom Forgave

In his writings the apostle Paul clearly teaches us the importance of getting rid of anger:

"'In your anger do not sin': Do not let the sun go down while you are still angry, and do not give the devil a foothold" (Ephesians 4:26-27).

Kit is a mom who learned the importance of asking the Holy Spirit's help to obey this admonition. After living in the Dallas area for a number of years, she, with her husband and family, moved to a 160-acre tract of land they had inherited in Louisiana. Kit and her husband were new Christians at the time, with an eight-year-old daughter and twelve-year-old son.

"I hadn't been thrilled about making the move, but for my son, Russell, it was a traumatic culture shock," Kit said. "We were 15 miles from the nearest town. No more playing tennis or swimming at the country club. The only possibility for swimming was in a rice canal that ran across the property."

As time went by and puberty set in, Russell became increasingly sullen and irritable. One afternoon as she was about to go into town, Kit discovered he had not done his assigned chores. When she questioned him about it, he shot back a sarcastic comment and started to walk out of the room.

"His attitude made me angry. He wouldn't have dared to speak to his father like that," she reported. "I reacted by slamming him against the kitchen wall. But I instantly realized that he was both taller and more muscular than I. He could hurt me! He leaned back against the wall with complete surprise in his eyes, as I had never reacted toward him in such a physical manner."

As Kit drove her car to town she talked to the Lord about her angry actions. The Holy Spirit gently reminded her that it was her duty to correct Russell, but that she had gone overboard in her response.

"When I got back home, I went to his bedroom door and knocked," she said. "The instant he opened the door I started to say, 'Russell, I am very sorry about the way I acted...' But before I could finish he broke in with, 'Mom, I'm the one who needs to say I'm sorry!' We hugged one another, and I cried with thanksgiving for the wonderful way the Holy Spirit handles our problems when we do things God's way."

Dealing with Anger

Many of us have had the frustrating experience of becoming angry with our children, and then later, if we were truly honest, acknowledging that the root of our animosity was not related to them at all. We simply took the opportunity to release our pent-up feelings when a child committed a minor infraction. Allowing this tendency to become a habitual pattern erodes a woman's spiritual life and sets a poor example for her children. But God's help is available to every one of us.

When Dorothy found herself lashing out in rage whenever her children began to feud about something, she realized she had a problem with buried anger she hadn't known was there. She began memorizing Scriptures on the subject, and she asked the Lord to help her control her own temper so she in turn could teach her children how to handle theirs. Gradually she learned the technique of giving her frustration to Jesus and taught her children to do the same.

One afternoon her five-year-old, Ben, socked his younger cousin, Sam, when he broke Ben's new favorite toy. Dorothy separated the boys and told Ben to ask Sam to forgive him for hitting him. Then she told Sam to ask Ben's forgiveness for breaking his toy. Both boys said, "Sorry." Then Dorothy explained to Sam that he and his mom would need to find a way to replace the broken toy.

Though Ben had asked Sam's forgiveness for smacking him and had accepted Sam's apology, he was still seething with anger.

"Go to your room, Ben, and give your anger to Jesus," Dorothy told her son. "Tell him you are sorry you lost your temper, and ask him to help you get it under control."

After a while he came back into the family room. "Mom, I gave Jesus my bad mood and asked for his peace," he said.

"Honey, that's good news," she replied. Then she used the experience to explain the Bible passage in Ephesians 4:2-3, turning it into a prayer: "Lord, I pray that my children will be humble and gentle, that they will be patient, and that they will love one another and attempt to live in peace." Ben is learning that whenever he loses his temper, he needs to go off by himself and talk to Jesus about it.

What Is Forgiveness?

Of course, all of us don't deal with the anger we occasionally feel toward our children as graciously as some moms are able to do. Before thinking it through, we sometimes react by speaking words we later wish we could erase. In her book *Easing the Pain of Parenthood*, Mary Rae Deatrick offers this advice for parents:

> Facing our emotions, facing facts, and accepting the circumstances opens the door to our casting the burden on the Lord in prayer. We are now ready to receive from God our comfort, our emotional healing, and our guidance...Let us correct what we can correct, change what we can change, and forgive all the mess that is left over. I beseech you not to think of failure as final.[2]

Kit's and Dorothy's examples clearly illustrate the fact that forgiveness is a decision, an act of one's will. Too often when one of our children does something that's irresponsible, devious, or rebellious, we allow anger to cloud our reason. Our emotions stand in the way of our being willing to forgive the offender. But God is faithful to remind us of our need to forgive, just as he has forgiven us.

The psalmist describes just how far God's forgiveness goes: "As far as the east is from the west, so far has he removed our transgressions from us" (Psalm 103:12). In considering the full meaning of forgiveness, we see the following steps as part of the process:

1. giving up the desire to punish or get even

2. excusing the offender for a fault or misdemeanor

3. turning from defensiveness

4. letting go of resentment

5. renouncing anger

6. absolving from payment

When we decide to take the first step toward forgiving a child's offense, we can access the power of the Holy Spirit to help us with the rest of the process. This doesn't mean we allow the child to "get away" with disobedience or bad behavior. We can ask the Lord to help us apply the appropriate discipline, but we can also use the situation to teach our child the power of God's mercy and forgiveness. These verses help us put the truth in perspective:

> Whenever you speak, or whatever you do, remember that you will be judged by the law of love, the law that set you free. For there will be no mercy for you if you have not been merciful to others. But if you have been merciful, then God's mercy toward you will win out over his judgment against you (James 2:12-13 NLT).

Keep on Forgiving

During the period when Debbie had four school-age children to get out the door every morning, it seemed that becoming angry with her kids was a part of her everyday routine.

"I'm not sure when my children's misbehavior stopped being a normal part of childhood that required correction and started being a catalyst for my temper," Debbie wrote. "My kids did so many things that angered me. Jim's arguing, Jerry's tattling, Julie's emotional outbursts, Janet's whining."

At first Debbie dismissed her flare-ups as a temporary result of cranky kids. But finally she faced the painful fact that she dreaded their arrival home from school. When she prayed about it, the Lord showed her she needed to forgive her children.

"Though I had asked God to forgive me for getting angry, I hadn't asked him to help me to forgive my children's insults," she said. "No wonder their first offense in the morning made me mad! I wanted to get rid of the burden of my children's yesterdays, so one day I gave their arguing, tattling, outbursts, and whining to God, and asked him to help me forgive as he does—with nothing left clinging. But immediately I thought, *I'm going to have to do this a thousand times before my kids are grown.*"[3]

When I (Quin) read Debbie's story I thought, *Dear Debbie, you'll have to keep on forgiving them even after they are grown! I know I have had to.*

Here's a heads-up from a seasoned mom: Just because you forgive once doesn't mean your child (or children) won't do the same thing to wound you again and again. But if you decide ahead of time that you will choose forgiveness over reacting in anger, you will be closer to your goal of becoming a Spirit-led mom. And it will create peace in your heart and home.

Corrie ten Boom, the renowned Dutch evangelist, had a unique way of explaining why it may take time to reach a place of total forgiveness, especially if you've been storing up a list of offenses against someone. She likened it to the sexton pulling a rope to ring the bell in a church tower. As long as he keeps yanking on the rope, the bell continues to ring. She writes:

> After the sexton lets go of the rope, the bell keeps on swinging. First ding, then dong. Slower and slower until there's a final dong and it stops. When we forgive someone, we take our hands off the rope. But if we've been tugging at our grievances for a long time, we mustn't be surprised when the old angry thoughts keep coming for a while. They're just the ding-dongs of the old bell slowing down.[4]

Yes, the accusing thoughts may keep ringing over and over in your mind for a while. But you can counteract those thoughts by obeying this Scripture: "We demolish arguments and every pretension that sets itself up against the knowledge of God, and we take captive every thought to make it obedient to Christ" (2 Corinthians 10:5).

Let's focus on God's promise to forgive us as we forgive those who offend us and then apply this promise to forgiving our children—even if it takes a while for our memory bank to stop preserving the evidence and for the final ding-dong to fade away.

Finding God's Help to Forgive

Dolores told us about her struggle with anger when her daughter informed her that her 13-year-old brother, Willie, was out in the woods with his friends smoking marijuana.

"I was dismayed," she said. "After all we'd taught him about staying off drugs, how could he? I needed to talk to someone, but I was ashamed to admit my failure to our friends and family. My husband, Steve, was unavailable. He worked at a construction job in the daytime and as an engineer at night, trying to catch us up financially after a long and devastating layoff. So I took matters into my own hands."

Setting off with the family dog to sniff out their exact where-abouts, she soon came upon the three teenagers sitting around a small campfire and staring into the flames. She saw no evidence of smoking when she arrived, so they must have heard her coming. But Dolores grabbed her son, jerked him to his feet, and marched him home while the other boys scattered.

"Why are you doing this to me?" she yelled when they got to his room. But she was trying to communicate with someone whose brain was fogged. He just stared at her without answering.

Dolores faced the reality that part of the situation was due to her and Steve's own negligence. Steve was gone most of the time, and on weekends he spent hours on the phone with his construction business. In self-defense, or more likely in retaliation, she had decided to pursue her long-deferred goal of getting an education. Wasn't 16 years of full-time childcare enough? She figured her two teenagers were old enough to fend for themselves in the evening while she drove 40 miles to the university for evening classes.

"After class, instead of going home, I would go out for pizza with a friend who was suffering from the breakup of her marriage," Dolores said. "My friend said our talks helped her; however, I was no help at all to my family."

Alarmed by her anger toward Willie, Dolores realized that drastic changes were needed, and that they would have to start with her. Instead of enrolling for the next semester at the university, she pursued a Bible study at her church. She learned the importance of having a personal relationship with God as her heavenly Father, and with Jesus as her Lord and Savior. And she discovered the value of spending time alone every day to pray, study the Scriptures, and seek the Holy Spirit's direction for her life.

During her studies she realized that God really did have something worthwhile and up to date to say to her personally through his Word. When Isaiah 55:8-9 in her Amplified Bible became very real to her one day, she marked it and wrote it in her note-book so she would never forget:

> My thoughts are not your thoughts, neither are your ways My ways, says the Lord. For as the heavens are higher than the earth, so are My ways higher than your ways and My thoughts than your thoughts.

"I believed that meant I could trust God to give me a kind of direction and guidance that I could never come up with on my own," Dolores said. "To help bring my anger under control, a verse in James also became my lifeline: 'Be quick to listen, slow to speak and slow to become angry, for man's anger does not bring about the righteous life that God desires' (James 1:19-20)."

As other Bible verses came alive to her, Dolores highlighted them and wrote them down until she had filled a small red velvet book. She called this little volume her "first-aid book" and turned to it frequently when she felt a spirit of hopelessness settling in. Besides finding promises from God and journaling her thoughts, Dolores began applying disciplines that would help her to walk in the counsel and power of the Holy Spirit for the rest of her life.

"I finally confessed that I was a poor mother, and I asked Jesus to forgive me for indulging my anger," she said. "That was primary to forgiving Willie for being such a difficult son. Even at that, I had to keep on forgiving him every single day. Every time I got angry at him I would pray, 'Lord, I know my anger will not make a righteous man out of my son. Only your power can do that.' God's promises were all I had to cling to. After years of struggle, Willie started turning to God to solve his problems."[5]

We moms often struggle with forgiving a disobedient child because we feel we must first apply some form of discipline. Are there instances when we should bypass the discipline and simply offer forgiveness? The next story gives an interesting insight on this question.

A Lesson in Forgiveness

Our friend Beth and her husband, Floyd, faced a hard choice about their oldest child. They discovered one Saturday that 14-year-old Julee and a neighbor's daughter had gone without permission on a "car date" with an older teenager, a kid who seemed like a bad influence.

Not knowing where their daughter had gone, Beth and Floyd walked the floor and prayed, asking God to put a hedge of protection around her. Later that evening, as Floyd was about to leave for his nightshift job, Julee called.

"Mom, can you come get me?" she asked plaintively.

"Where are you? I'll be there right away," Beth answered.

Before leaving, she and Floyd talked over how to handle the matter. They reminded themselves that if Julee asked for their forgiveness, they would need to give it. But they also would call a family council to discuss what had happened. When they drove both their cars to the address, they found Julee sitting on the curb, anxiously waiting for them.

"I'll see you at family council tomorrow. Right now I've got to go to work," Floyd told her. He drove off, leaving Beth to cope with a very distraught teenager.

"Mom, I didn't do anything, honest!" Julee cried, falling into her mother's arms.

"You get in the car and wait for me," Beth replied sternly. She went inside the unfamiliar house and was horrified to find the place filled with spaced-out teenagers. Liquor bottles and burnt-out marijuana joints were everywhere. Finding her neighbor's daughter, she pulled her outside and led her to the car.

"Don't say a word to me right now," Beth said, struggling to control her anger as she drove the girls back across town. "I need time to think this through."

Julee cried all the way to her friend's house. After the other girl had gone inside, Julee blurted out, "Mom, will you forgive me?"

"Yes, I will," Beth answered, though she really didn't feel very forgiving at the time.

"Will Daddy forgive me?" Julee asked, still weeping.

"You'll have to ask him. Want to write him a note?"

After they arrived at their house, Julee scrawled on a sheet of notebook paper, "Daddy, I'm sorry. Will you forgive me? Love, Julee," and left it on the dining room table. After he had come home from work and gone to bed, she came out of her room to find his response.

With great relief she read, "I forgive you. Love, Dad."

Meanwhile, as they prepared for the family council, Floyd and Beth decided they would deal with the matter by teaching Julee a lesson in unconditional forgiveness.

What About Yesterday?

The next day Floyd and Beth and their three girls sat around the table for their council meeting. "Does anyone need to discuss anything this morning?" Floyd asked. He glanced around the circle. "Beth, do you have anything to bring up?"

"No, I don't," she answered, shaking her head.

"What about yesterday?" Julee asked anxiously, looking from one parent to the other.

"What about yesterday?" Floyd asked.

"Daddy...you know!" Julee exclaimed.

"No, I don't know," he answered, handing her his Bible and a slip of paper. "Now, Julee, please read our devotional. I've written out these references for today."

Opening her dad's Bible, Julee read before the entire family:

> When you stand praying, if you hold anything against anyone, forgive him, so that your Father in heaven may forgive you your sins (Mark 11:25).

> Do not grieve the Holy Spirit of God.... Get rid of all bitterness, rage and anger, brawling and slander, along

with every form of malice. Be kind and compassionate to one another, forgiving each other, just as in Christ God forgave you (Ephesians 4:30-32).

Peter came to Jesus and asked, "Lord, how many times shall I forgive my brother when he sins against me? Up to seven times?" Jesus answered, "I tell you, not seven times, but seventy-seven times" (Matthew 18:21-22).

Julee was completely disarmed by her parents' act of total for-giveness. As she read the verses of Scripture, she and her sisters wept. Floyd closed the meeting with prayer, thanking God for his love and forgiveness. They never again mentioned Julee's disobedience.

An Apology

One day almost a year later, a nice-looking young man knocked on their door and asked to speak with Beth. "You don't know me, but I'm the one who took your daughter off to a pot party last summer," he explained. "I had joined the church youth group in order to meet young, innocent kids like Julee and intro-duce them to drugs. The idea was to get them hooked so they would depend on us for their supply."

Beth invited him to come in and sit down to tell the rest of the story.

"Your 14-year-old daughter wouldn't try anything at that party," he continued. "When she asked, I refused to take her home, and that's when she called you. I was angry that a 14-year-old girl had more self-control than I did at 18. I began searching for meaning in my life after that, and I finally found it in Jesus Christ. Now I'm working for Jesus, trying to snatch young people out of the drug culture. But I apologize to you for what happened with Julee last summer."

How glad Beth and Floyd were that they had reacted to their daughter's disobedience with love and forgiveness! Not only was it a valuable lesson for Julee, but also for her younger sisters—and never again did one of them leave the house on a date without permission.

Maybe you have not yet had to face an issue like this one, but the biblical principles other Spirit-led parents share for dealing with problems can inspire us to go to the Scriptures for solutions to our own challenges.

For instance, I (Quin) saw a passage of Scripture in a new light when my friend Sylvia told me how she learned to forgive her son, Matthew. Over the years I've used her "method" when I have needed to forgive someone. As your children grow older and you have to deal with forgiveness issues, you also may find Sylvia's example very useful.

Charge It to Jesus

Though Matthew was no longer living at home, when he would drop by for visits Sylvia dreaded to see him walk in her front door because he would make such a horrible scene. After shouting and calling her names, he'd angrily speed away down the driveway. She, in turn, would collapse in tears.

For years Sylvia had depended on the Holy Spirit to give her answers. One afternoon after her son's visit she sat out on her patio, Bible in hand, for an honest talk with the Lord. "God, I hurt so badly when Matthew says such ugly things to me. I'm having a hard time forgiving him for all his wounding words."

Opening her Bible, she read the book of Philemon, Paul's letter to a friend asking him to take back his runaway slave, who had become a Christian under Paul's ministry. These words seemed to leap straight into her heart: "If he has done you any wrong or owes you anything, charge it to me...I will pay it back—not to mention that you owe me your very self" (Philemon 18-19).

Jesus seemed to whisper to her, *If Matthew has done any wrong or owes you anything, charge it to me. I will pay it back. But don't forget, you owe me your very life.* These words gave Sylvia a practical way to deal with her hurt. She poured out her heart to the Lord that day, charging all Matthew's insults to Jesus' account.

"I forgave my son and asked God to forgive him too," she said. "In so doing I released Matthew from having consciously or unconsciously inflicted all those wounds on me through the years. Then I thanked God for allowing me to be his mother, for I had adopted him when he was quite small."[6]

Today, Matthew not only is walking with the Lord, he leads a home Bible study once a week, and his mom is always there to encourage him.

Choosing to Forgive

Paul writes, "Be kind and compassionate to one another, forgiving each other, just as in Christ God forgave you" (Ephesians 4:32). In this verse, the word *forgiving* in the original Greek means "to bestow a favour unconditionally."[7] Forgiving, by God's plan, is to freely bestow favor on the one who has offended us. Jesus clearly instructed us: "Forgive, and you will be forgiven" (Luke 6:37). Here, forgive means to "let loose from" or "to release, set at liberty."[8]

When we choose to forgive a person, several things are set in motion:

1. We extend love and mercy to the one forgiven.

2. We release him from our judgment and allow God to do the judging.

3. We free both ourselves and the other person from the bondage of unforgiveness.

4. With a clean heart, we can now pray for that person to receive God's blessings.

5. We will be able to receive the blessings which come when we obey God's Word.

As soon as we realize that our words or thoughtless reactions have hurt our children, we need to do something about it. However, it is important to pray for the right timing and the right words, and to be sure that when we ask a child to forgive us, we're doing it with the right motive and an attitude of humility.

By setting such an example, we will teach our children one of the most powerful and significant life lessons they will ever learn.

Prayer

You may find one of the following prayers appropriate for your situation:

Father, please prepare my child to receive my apology. Help me to speak honestly, but with your love and compassion. I trust you to prepare the opportunity for forgiveness and reconciliation to take place. Thank you, Lord, that you will give us victory in this situation and heal our relationship. Thank you for forgiving me and for forgiving my child. In Jesus' name, amen.

Or

Father, give me the ability to forgive my child. I ask for your wisdom and strength and discernment. I pray the Holy Spirit will be my teacher and comforter as I walk through this hurtful incident. Help me to appropriate your grace to overrule my own disappointment, resentment, or desire to punish harshly. Thank you that Romans 5:5 assures me that you will pour your love into my heart by the Holy Spirit, giving me the capacity to love my child more profoundly than ever before. Lord, I want my actions to be pleasing to you. Amen.

Scriptures for Meditation

"Forgive us our debts, as we also have forgiven our debtors" (Matthew 6:12).

"Do not judge, and you will not be judged. Do not condemn, and you will not be condemned. Forgive, and you will be forgiven" (Luke 6:37).

"I [Paul] have forgiven in the sight of Christ for your sake, in order that Satan might not outwit us. For we are not unaware of his schemes" (2 Corinthians 2:10-11).

8
Power for the Pressures of Life
Calming Life's Frantic Pace

There remains, then, a Sabbath-rest for the people of God;
for anyone who enters God's rest also rests from his
own work, just as God did from his. Let us, therefore,
make every effort to enter that rest.
—HEBREWS 4:9-11

Oh, my slice of time alone has certainly not been the magic solution
to everything. I still can't load the kids into the van faster than a
speeding bullet or leap over tall agendas at a single bound.
But I can do something even better. I can laugh more easily.
Live more lightly. Enjoy things just as they are a little more often.
I can remember that there is a whole lot more to this mommy than
mere movement. I can even dare to believe—one nap,
one prayer, one pause at a time—that I really don't
have to earn love by proving my usefulness.[1]
—DEENA LEE WILSON

oday's world is a busy place filled with activities and obligations for most families—many of them suffering from activity overload. Yet God wants us to rest in his love, to "be" rather than to "do."

The above verses from Hebrews set before us the promise of that elusive treasure so many stressed moms only dream about—*rest*. Because the verb *to rest* means to cease from labor, we generally associate it with physical rest. But we want to look at the idea of *rest* in a broader way—having an inner sense of God's peace and the ability to fulfill our responsibilities without feeling numb or frazzled by the end of the day.

Through Christ's provision for us, we have the opportunity to enter into his rest—a place of utter dependence upon God. But too often we moms try to manage our duties and pressures on our own, forgetting that God's rest is available. We need to modify our endless cycle of activity and adopt God's perspective, remembering that God is not, never has been, and never will be pressured or in a hurry.

His Burden Is Light

I (Ruthanne) remember a stressful time in my life when I attended a spring weekend retreat at a guest ranch in the Texas hills. The schedule allowed ample opportunity for meditation and reflection, which I sorely needed at the time.

One afternoon I climbed a hill to a large, flat rock and sat down to enjoy the expansive view in the warm sunshine. I told the Lord how frustrated I was with the conflict I felt between challenges I faced with my 12-year-old son and the pressure of a writing assignment I had accepted. *How can I do everything that's expected of me?* I questioned.

As I prayed the Holy Spirit reminded me of Jesus' words: "Come to me, all you who are weary and burdened, and I will give you rest…For my yoke is easy and my burden is light" (Matthew 11:28,30). When I realized the pressure I was feeling was a burden of my own making, I repented for trying to do things in my own strength. I determined to leave my burden on that huge rock and to rely more completely on the Holy Spirit's help and guidance for every task and family problem.

I returned home the next day feeling refreshed and energized. Had the circumstances changed? Not really. But I looked at them differently now. And I better understood what it meant to "make every effort to enter that rest" (Hebrews 4:11). Effort is required as you resist doing things your own way and try to establish the habit of drawing upon God's strength so the demands of life don't weigh you down.

Now my husband and I live in the Texas hill country, and I have a great stress reliever at hand when I feel the pressure of trying to do too many things in too little time. I can sit on the back porch of our log home, watching the deer and enjoying the view as I ask the Lord to help me order my priorities. But I still have to make the effort to lay my work aside and take a breather if I want to avoid being exhausted by the end of the day.

What Are Your Priorities?

A Spirit-led mom is one who somehow finds the power to help her family find peace with its own healthy pace while withstanding the pressures to get caught up with unnecessary busyness. But how? She must take inventory and decide what is really important in helping her youngsters develop into good, well-rounded kids. But mainly, she must establish her own "resting place"—her solitary time to pray, reflect, and find direction from God.

We asked several Christian moms what they consider to be priorities for their families. Here are some of their answers:

- ♪ praying together and going to church as a family

- ♪ eating at least one meal a day together as a family

- ♪ not overloading little ones with pressures they can't handle

- ♪ scheduling time for her spouse (a date)

- ♪ making room for some quiet time for herself

⮞ maintaining prayer partner friendships and keeping appointments with them

My (Quin's) daughter Quinett told me the other day, "Mom, I've found I pray a lot as I iron clothes, vacuum the carpet, do the dishes, and drive to the grocery store. Some of my friends complain they can't find an hour a day to pray, but there's plenty of time if they would just pray 'minute prayers' while they work." I agree!

Before her five- and seven-year-old leave for school, she stands with them in front of the refrigerator or "prayer board" where photos of their relatives and friends are posted. Not only do they pray for those pictured there, but they pray for themselves for the day—that they will have good attitudes, the ability to listen and learn, and to have favor with their teachers. They also pray that they will maintain healthy bodies. This last issue is especially important for the five-year-old, who has asthma.

Twice a month Quinett meets her best friend for tea. While exchanging prayer requests and recipes, they laugh over the silly incidents that happen in families. She's a busy mom, but she knows she has to schedule time for herself too.

Learning to Flow Together

Working moms we've talked with said they must guard from putting unrealistic expectations on their families when they're holding down jobs to contribute to the family income. "I do this because my kids wouldn't be getting music lessons, gymnastics, or ballet if I didn't pay for it," one mom told us. Another said she realized she had to change her attitude and habits to help her family adjust to her new work schedule.

"When I decided to go back to teaching this year, I knew I couldn't put my family under the same pressure as before," says Carla, mom to an eight-year-old daughter and ten-year-old son. "The Holy Spirit seemed to urge me that to keep us all from being stressed-out, I needed to get as organized as possible. As an aside, he also encouraged me to walk out of my bedroom each morning with a smile on my face. It has worked. I try to do housework and laundry on week nights and save the weekends for our family fun times."

Carla looks on her job as an opportunity to show Christ's love to the mostly underprivileged children she teaches at a public elementary school. Her work hours allow her to arrive home around the same time as her kids so she can drive her son to Little League or her daughter to soccer, if necessary.

"We've learned to flow together even more as a family since I've gone back to teaching, but like all families, it took a while for us to adjust," she said with a laugh. "Each morning before I leave for my teaching job, I ask God for what I call my 'today anointing' and trust him to map out my day. Of course the day does flow more smoothly both at school and at home when I do that, so I won't miss my prayer time. Sundays always find us in church together."

Seek First His Kingdom

Allotting some time for quiet and "down time" requires that we unplug our minds from guilt, worry, and fear and just rest! Too often, we moms respond to the guilt that assails us rather than listening to God's still, small voice. Baskets of clothes wait to be washed. Beds aren't made. Dishes are soaking in the sink. The stock of groceries is low. Dinner needs to be prepared. All these things make us feel that, even if we are exhausted, we have to push ahead.

I (Quin) cannot remember a time when I was raising three children that I just stopped to take a nap. It never occurred to me that I'd be a better mom if I rested for half an hour on days when I was drained. Looking back, I realize that I did do one thing that greatly relaxed me and brought my children pleasure too. I'd drop just about anything I was doing to take them to the beach. My son said I was the only mom in the neighborhood they could count on to drive them to the ocean so they could surf.

While waiting for them to catch the next perfect wave, I'd walk the white sand beaches as the wind, pounding surf, and salt air helped me relax. Even better, my soul was refreshed as I talked with the Lord during those walks. Today I can still close my eyes and picture those wonderful sun-filled afternoons spent on the Florida beaches I love so much. And I smile with gratitude about the promises God gave me for my children during our seaside talks—promises which have now come to pass.

So many moms have a sense of failure about not spending adequate time in prayer. Our friend Diana Hagee, a busy pastor's wife who has raised five children, shares candidly her own experience of struggling to find time to pray. "I felt certain God had forgotten my name," she said. In her frustration she sought advice from her mother-in-law, whom she looked to as a mentor.

"Ask yourself if you are giving him all the time you can," Mrs. Hagee suggested. She also reminded Diana to stop comparing herself with other people because God doesn't do that with us. She assured Diana that God would reveal to her his answer and show her how she could rearrange her schedule to create time to talk to him. Then she advised her to use Jesus' instructions for prayer as her guideline (see Matthew 6:5-15).

Diana says she followed this advice and began talking to God as a daughter to a loving Father. "I did not lock myself in a closet and stay away from my daily chores, but I took my prayer closet with me...Sometimes my prayers were long conversations or simply two or three words. One of the most powerful prayers I prayed was, 'Lord, intervene!' "[2]

Being a Spirit-led mom gives us plenty of opportunity to be involved in the lives of our family members. But being a hurried, harried mom is not God's plan for us. Jesus didn't hurry through life. If we would but heed his timeless counsel about priorities, other things would fall into place in God's way and in his timing:

Therefore I tell you, do not worry about your life, what you will eat or drink; or about your body, what you will wear. Is not life more important than food, and the body more important than clothes?...But seek first his kingdom and his righteousness, and all things will be given to you as well (Matthew 6:25,33).

So Much to Do!

Author Cheri Fuller admits that with the addition of each of her children her schedule became more and more hectic. She was supervising homework and school and sports activities, juggling writing deadlines, volunteering at church, and helping in her husband's business. The sense of wonder she had once shared with her little ones was replaced by work and worries. "I was missing the small miracles God placed along my path," she writes. "I wanted to share in my children's joy and sense of discovery...but there was so much to do!"[3]

Cheri shares her experience:

Finally, quite frustrated, I asked God, "What can I do?"

Quietly He seemed to whisper, *"Go fly a kite!"*

"Oh, Lord," I replied, "that seems so silly and impractical."

"That's the point!" He responded.

So I went to the toy store and bought a kite to fly at our next family outing in the park. Chris and Justin enjoyed the challenge of getting the kite up to catch the breeze, and Alison loved having her turn to fly it, but eventually they all got bored and ran off to play. I was left holding the string.

As the bright red and blue kite swept up and flew almost out of sight, my spirits soared. The breeze blew my hair, and a fresh sense of wonder blew over my heart. I forgot all the things I needed to accomplish and reveled in the blue sky, the huge cascade of clouds. Then, as I gazed up, there it was! A spectacular double rainbow! A double promise, a double blessing.

Flying the kite not only refreshed my spirit but pointed me upward, toward God, who knew what would make my heart sing.[4]

Most of us have a special something that makes our hearts sing—an activity that refreshes us and imparts renewed energy when we take a few moments to indulge in it.

Carrie sits out on her deck several evenings a week to soak up the beauty of the sun setting behind the mountains near her home. Bonnie takes a bike ride to let the breeze blow the cobwebs from her mind. Joanna finds solace in the hot tub at the YMCA once a week. Billie writes down one "heart's desire" she plans to achieve in the coming week that will add adventure to her life and break her routine.

If you have put off thinking about a special activity you would enjoy because you're just too occupied with everyday duties, stop and write down that "heart's desire." Then ask the Lord to help you find a window of time to take pleasure from it.

Saving Time for God

Connie is an example of a busy Spirit-led mom of three—a toddler, a five-year-old, and a seven-year-old. Yet in the midst of her family's busyness, she "schedules" a quiet time for herself daily.

Her husband, an ex-athlete, wants the older boys to participate in sports, and both of them want their children involved in church activities. So five nights a week they are engaged in one event or another. Depending on the season, the family shuttles back and forth to hockey games, ball games, or swimming. Sundays they attend church, and one night a month Connie teaches a Bible study.

But this wise mom uses her baby's nap time for her time with the Lord while her boys are in school. During the summer, the boys play quiet games in their rooms while the baby naps and Connie prays, studies the Bible, and worships the Lord. They never answer the phone or the doorbell during this time. Then Connie prepares an early supper for the family to enjoy together before they go off for sporting events.

Before the boys leave for school in the mornings, she prays over them. Sometimes they listen to children's praise tapes while they eat breakfast. "This seems to have a calming effect on them and on me," she says. She does have a short prayer time before the rest of the family awakens in the mornings, but her main "study" time with God is in the afternoons.

A former school teacher who is proficient in music, Connie wants her two sons to learn to play at least one instrument, but she's put that dream on hold for now. In the meantime, she exposes them to good music on CDs. When they are older she will find a way to add lessons to their schedule.

As the children grow and develop, Connie will have to adapt her own routine accordingly. But knowing how important it is for her to have time with God, this will remain a high priority. Since we all have different "time clocks" and family schedules, we must experiment and learn what works best for our current season of life. These words from Oswald Chambers can help us evaluate what is truly important:

> Do crises which affect us or others in our home, business, country, or elsewhere seem to be crushing in on us? Are we being pushed out of the presence of God and left with no time for worship?...Beware of getting ahead of God by your very desire to do His will. We run ahead of Him in a thousand and one activities,

becoming so burdened with people and problems that we don't worship God, and we fail to intercede. If a burden and its resulting pressure come upon us while we are not in an attitude of worship, it will only produce a hardness toward God and despair in our own souls.[5]

Let's be honest. Most of us from time to time need to stop and reconnect with the things that are on God's heart for us and for our families.

Nothing Is Too Difficult for God

Today's moms find that life's stresses come in all sizes and designs. But for many divorced moms, the additional problem of dealing with custody issues compounds the pressure—both for them and for the children involved.

Teresa wrote us about sharing the custody of their five-year-old son, Danny, with her ex-husband. The divorce courts in their state gave parents equal time with minor children. This meant Danny spent three days each week with his dad and then four with his mom.

Was the arrangement fair to Danny? Teresa pondered that question often. She began seeing signs that her son was suffering because of continually moving from one home to another and never feeling that he truly belonged anywhere. It hurt her deeply to see how the strain was becoming almost overwhelming for him.

"My biggest nightmare was that I might lose my son," she said. "But after praying about it, I finally mustered the courage to tell my ex-husband of my concerns. Though neither of us wanted to give up time with Danny, I didn't want to go to court, as the judge might rule either way. Every thought of the possibility of losing Danny made me sick inside and the tears would flow. I was desperate to hear from God and to have his peace."

As Teresa continued in prayer, the Lord showed her that her situation was much like the story of two women who brought a baby to King Solomon and asked him to settle their dispute over who was the real mother. He proposed cutting the baby in two and giving half to each woman. One woman protested, insisting the child be given to her adversary—which of course revealed that indeed she was the rightful mother (see 1 Kings 3:16-28).

"It became clear to me that a mother who loves and desires the best for her child must choose life for him, even if it means not being able to raise him," Teresa said. "I realized our son was being ripped in two. It was very difficult, but I had to put aside my personal desires and do what was best for Danny. After more prayer and soul-searching, I told the Lord if I had to release my son to live with his father, I would.

"When I phoned my ex-husband again to try to reach an agreement, we had quite a discussion, but in the end he consented to allow Danny to live with me. What a miracle! Only God could have turned this man's heart and caused him to become willing to give up his rights in this way. Through this experience I learned that God truly honors integrity, and nothing is too difficult for him."

Danny's parents did work out a compatible visitation schedule for holidays and summers to give him special time with his dad.

Other moms have different sorts of pressure that seem to push them to the brink.

When Mary Ann gave up her nursing career to care for her three preschoolers, she missed conversing with adult friends. So she set up one room in the house as a playroom and then invited other moms with preschoolers to come over on certain days. The moms enjoyed visiting while supervising the kids at play. Occasionally she would invite several couples to bring their children and come for dinner, but she asked them to bring their favorite potluck dish. Everyone welcomed these inexpensive, fun evenings of fellowship.

Lynn, a homeschooling mom of three stair-step children, struggled with how to fit grocery shopping into her schedule. Her husband was gone all day with their only car, and trying to do it on weekends was way too stressful. Her answer was to plan her major shopping on a night when Dad could be at home with the kids after they were ready for bed. Thus she was free to shop at a nearby 24-hour supermarket at a time when the store wasn't crowded, traffic was light, and she could browse the aisles at leisure.

Regardless of the source of the stress we feel, the solution is to slow down, evaluate our situation, and ask the Holy Spirit to show us how we can calm our frantic pace.

Observe the Speed Limit

Why do we think we can run like a steam locomotive all the time? God himself worked six days and then rested on the seventh. One of the commandments he gave to Moses was to remember the Sabbath (see Exodus 20:8-11). God did not create our bodies to run 18 or 20 hours a day, every day of the year. If we try to keep that pace, we will find ourselves falling apart.

Once I (Quin) was asked to do yet another volunteer task as a room mother. I was a working mom with three children in that elementary school. "Sorry, that's not my expertise," I told the teacher. It was true. I had no talent at all for the things she wanted done by a room mother. But it was the first time I had been bold enough to say no to a teacher without feeling guilty. Had I taken on that project, my entire family would have been affected by my frustration.

Ask yourself what you can do to lighten your workload to make you a better, happier, more compatible woman (wife, mom, career person). Maybe it is saying no to the Cub Scout troop this year, or buying cookies instead of baking them for the first-grade class. It may mean enjoying a hot bath with no kids around for one whole hour. Or spending a quiet evening out with your husband. Decide what you want to do to bring balance to your life and then take steps toward making it happen. You could stop for a moment and ask yourself these questions:

- ❧ What are my priorities right now? (Be honest as you list them.)

- ❧ Am I doing anything now that the Lord wants me to give up? If so, how can I make a plan to do that? (Ask God for the strategy.)

- ❧ How can I find more time for worship and studying God's Word?

- ❧ What are my God-given dreams? (Don't be afraid to list them, and give yourself a timetable. Be faithful in doing little things to help you achieve those dreams.)

Enjoy Your Children, for This Will Pass

Achieving your God-given dreams is a wonderful goal, but sometimes, when the children seem to be always underfoot, you've just got to ask God for power to handle the pressures of the moment. When I (Quin) still had three children under the age of four I sometimes wondered, "Will I always be just a mommy to crying children with runny noses? Will there never be time for me to write articles again? Will I always feel tired, stressed, and at the beck and call of my children?"

After being up most of the night with a colicky baby, I was complaining to God about my ho-hum life one day. As I rocked the baby I heard God's whisper, *Embrace and enjoy this season, for it is a gift from me. Too quickly it will pass.* Put in that perspective, I realized God had confidence in me to rear these children. It was a high calling. I could defer my dream of having time to write while I concentrated on my role of motherhood.

"Lord, help me put first things first," I prayed.

My complaining stopped. I asked God for strength and endurance as I hung 22 diapers on the line early each morning before the kids woke up. We couldn't afford a clothes dryer and disposable diapers were not on the market. Looking back, I wouldn't trade all those moments I spent alone with the Lord for a dryer or throw-away diapers. As the breeze brushed my face and I watched dawn break across the sky, those backyard prayers and a sense of God's presence prepared me for the pressures I would face later in that day.

Learning to Set Boundaries for Yourself

Nan, a Spirit-led mom who is now a grandmother, looks back over her child-rearing years and writes this advice for her three daughters who are now raising their own children:

- Rest is a command.

- "No" is a holy word.

- Put boundaries around yourself, your time, and your schedule. Stick to them.

- Have "safety zones"—places of refuge from pressure, people, work, and agendas.

- Escape to them when necessary. Routinely. Daily.

- Learn how to rest—mentally, physically, and emotionally.

- If you can realize that nothing will ever be perfect, then the pressure is off you as a mom.

- We all have limitations. Learn to live with them.

- Seek God's help to obey his command not to worry, fret, or carry burdens.

- Lay those cares on Christ. Learn to trust him. He is God, we are not.

Tammy is a mom with young daughters who shared with us her observations:

> I think one of the biggest problems I've seen in mothers is that women today are overcommitted to too many things. For myself, I am a wife, a mom, a minister of music, and a private music instructor. "Spare time" is almost nonexistent in my life. Sometimes women can even be involved in too many Bible studies or prayer meetings at the expense of spending quality time with the Lord. Time alone with God is vitally important to being an example of Christ's character to your family.
>
> God has been dealing with me to step back and reevaluate my priorities and my schedule, including telephone time! My daughter really lets me know she needs my attention if I've been on the phone too long. God is putting a desire in me as never before to follow the example of the woman in Proverbs 31, but I know I cannot do that with everything I am committed to right now. Even "ministry" has to be given up to a degree. My husband and children should be my number one ministry responsibility. If I do not have time left for them, all my ministry activity is in vain.

Tammy is wise to make her daughters a priority while they're still young and let some of her ministry activities wait until her children are older. It's a decision she will never regret further down the road.

Probably all of us need to evaluate whether our lives are balanced in the areas of work, rest, worship, and play. As we learn how to hear and obey God's voice, he will show us ways to avoid overcommitting or overextending ourselves so that we can enter into his rest.

Prayer

Lord, I admit I sometimes overcommit myself. It is hard to say no to some things when I'm asked, even to activities I don't have any talent for or any business accepting on my overcrowded plate. Please help me in this area to be honest and even bold in saying no once in a while. Help me find balance—the right rhythm to my life—instead of needlessly overworking my body so that it wears out too soon. When I have finished my race I want to hear you say, "Well done, good and faithful servant" (Matthew 25:21).

Scriptures for Meditation

"The LORD is my shepherd, I shall not be in want. He makes me lie down in green pastures, he leads me beside quiet waters, he restores my soul" (Psalm 23:1-3).

"He who dwells in the shelter of the Most High will rest in the shadow of the Almighty. I will say of the LORD, 'He is my refuge and my fortress, my God, in whom I trust'" (Psalm 91:1-2).

"The Counselor, the Holy Spirit, whom the Father will send in my name, will teach you all things and will remind you of everything I have said to you. Peace I leave with you; my peace I give to you" (John 14:25-27).

"Do not be anxious about anything, but in everything, by prayer and petition, with thanksgiving, present your requests to God.

And the peace of God, which transcends all understanding, will guard your hearts and your minds in Christ Jesus" (Philippians 4:6-7).

"He mounted the cherubim and flew; he soared on the wings of the wind...the LORD was my support. He brought me out into a spacious place...because he delighted in me" (2 Samuel 22:11, 19-20).

9
Power for Healing
Praying for Physical and Emotional Well-Being

*Is anyone among you sick? Let him call for the elders of
the church, and let them pray over him, anointing him with
oil in the name of the Lord. And the prayer of faith will
save the sick, and the Lord will raise him up. And if he
has committed sins, he will be forgiven.*
—JAMES 5:14-15 NKJV

*Doubt sees the obstacles,
Faith sees the way;
Doubt sees the blackest night,
Faith sees the day;
Doubt dreads to take a step,
Faith soars on high;
Doubt questions, "Who believes?"
Faith answers, "I."*[1]
—AUTHOR UNKNOWN

very mother covets a healthy body, mind, and spirit for
her child. Yet when sickness, chronic disease, accidents,
emotional problems, or handicaps steal a child's health
and vitality, the Spirit-led mom finds herself on her knees more
than ever before. We want to give you encouragement and practical examples to help you cope with these issues and to pray
more effectively.

Of course, a mom who responds to the Holy Spirit's leading will lay a strong foundation of prayer for her children *before* an emergency occurs. Then when a health crisis does come, she knows that prayer is her first course of action.

But whether healing comes instantly, progressively, or hand in hand with medical treatment, we can always acknowledge God's handiwork in restoring a body. When a life-threatening illness struck six-year-old Gabby, her Spirit-led mom saw God at work at every level.

"He Told Me He Was Healing Me"

For several weeks the family doctor had treated Gabby for sinus infections and a runny nose. Five days after her last exam, Deb took her daughter back to the doctor. "I'm not leaving until I find out what is really wrong with my child," she said emphatically. Back to the examination table. But this time the doctor saw something incredulous—a tumor so big it was growing out of the child's nose.

"A very aggressive form of cancer called Rhabdo Myosarcoma," the doctor told Deb after running some tests. "You should take her immediately to say goodbye to her little sister."

Gabby laid her head in her mother's lap. "Am I going to die, Mommy?"

"No. No. No! We are praying," Deb answered.

Deb and her husband, Todd, immediately drove Gabby to a children's hospital in Phoenix two hours away. The oncologist there who took her case was no more optimistic. That night Gabby's heart stopped beating and she stopped breathing, but they were able to resuscitate her. Back at home, a group from their church met to pray, and about 20 of them drove to Phoenix to keep a prayer vigil for the ailing child.

The next day they wheeled Gabby into surgery for a biopsy. Doctors expected to find that the tumor had spread throughout her nervous system, but thankfully, they learned that was not the case.

"They still could not promise us anything hopeful, though," Deb remembers. "The tumor was so large. They couldn't operate because it filled all her sinus cavities. Even though there was no proven treatment for such a tumor, the next day doctors began radiation, followed by chemotherapy. They put an opening in her throat to aid her breathing. Several times we almost lost her again, but medical treatment and prayer worked together to keep her alive."

Deb says she stood on this promise: "I am still confident of this: I will see the goodness of the LORD in the land of the living" (Psalm 27:13).

One day when the nurse on Gabby's case told Deb the child could live only a few more hours, this determined mom went out into the "healing garden" on the hospital grounds to pray while her mother-in-law kept bedside watch.

"I was confident that because my daughter knew the Lord Jesus, death for her was not a final thing," Deb said. "Yet I desperately believed God's plan was for her to live. That afternoon I shouted aloud, 'The enemy cannot have her. She is covered with the blood of Jesus. If she dies, the good Lord will have her escorted home to heaven.'"

Then she declared, "Lord, I believe you have given me your promise that you are going to heal her. I am going to praise you in advance for that."

Deb went back into the hospital, fell asleep near Gabby's bedside, and enjoyed the first night of complete rest she'd had for several days. The next morning she awoke to find her daughter sitting on the edge of the bed, asking for food. Since entering the hospital, she'd had nothing but liquids fed to her through an IV tube.

Later, Gabby told her mother that that night she saw Jesus come into her room and crawl up on her bed. "He told me he was healing me," she said.

Many more months of treatments followed. Because the tumor didn't shrink, the doctors decided to operate. They had to put her into a drug-induced coma and take a vein from her leg to reroute her blood supply to her head. If she came out of that coma, they would take her back to surgery to remove the tumor. This part was very scary, for she had a slim chance of survival, and even if she did survive, there was the possibility of brain damage. But Gabby surprised the entire medical staff and came out of the coma. So it was back to surgery again, this time to try to cut out the nasty thing that had invaded her head.

During the surgery her parents prayed that the doctors would be able to get the tumor and all its roots. Finally, a doctor brought them the good news: They had found the tumor's point of origin. They got the roots. They got everything. It was a time of great rejoicing for answered prayer.

Believing for the Future

Deb said one of the hardest aspects of Gabby's sickness was being away from her other daughter, two-year-old Grace. While Mom stayed in Phoenix at the hospital, Dad had to run the family business back home and tend to Grace. Sometimes between hospital visits, the toddler would show great resentment over Deb being gone so much.

"The standard in our home is to demonstrate the fruit of the Spirit," Deb said. "We couldn't allow either of our girls to become spoiled children. We wanted them to have God's character. So when I'd arrive home after dealing with life-and-death situations at the hospital and find that Grace was upset with me, I would tell her, 'I am your mom and I love you, but you can't get by with temper tantrums.' Whenever Gabby was able, I'd ask her to help with things around the house, like putting napkins on the table or emptying a garbage can. I have encouraged my daughters to become best friends, and today I think they are."

Even when Gabby was at her worst physically, Deb would remind herself to believe God for her future. Todd clung to a Scripture God had dropped into his heart for his daughter: "But unto you that fear My name shall the Sun of righteousness arise with healing in His wings" (Malachi 4:2 KJV). He firmly believed healing was coming.

"Each of us in his own way was dealing with what our family was going through," Deb remembers. "My husband held in his heart the vision of her future wedding day. I, on the other hand, tried to console a disappointed little girl who had no hair and wanted a thick mane. So I'd pray with Gabby for hair. We saw God's faithfulness through every step of the process."

Gabby's ordeal of healing took almost a year as she checked in and out of the hospital, with her mom homeschooling her whenever possible. Today she is a normal ten-year-old going into sixth grade. She even skipped a grade at school due to her homeschooling. Obviously the tumor did not affect her brain. The Lord indeed healed her, but he did it with the aid of modern medicine along with blankets of prayer.

God Cares About Details

Deb knew she had to rely on the help of the Holy Spirit in dealing with the long-term, life-threatening crisis she faced with Gabby. But we don't have to be confronting a life-and-death issue in order to have the Holy Spirit's help. Even with lesser health problems, God's resources are available to us. Nothing is too insignificant in our children's lives to get his notice, as the mom in this story discovered.

Eleanor was a Christian who knew God cared about her family, but she had a child with a very special need. Could she trust God to intervene? After hearing me (Quin) speak on prayer at a meeting in Alabama, Eleanor realized there were three things she needed to do:

1. give God quality prayer time

2. pray with specific requests

3. allow God to speak to her through his Word

She left that meeting with a burning desire to pray and a definite plan for how to do it.

Problem: Eugene, her 13-year-old adopted son, had not grown even an eighth of an inch in a year. At first she thought perhaps he was small of stature because of his Asian heritage, but then her doctor told her to take him to a specialist who would prescribe growth hormones.

Plan: Eleanor's habit for years had been to rise at 4:30 A.M. and run for several miles. Then she would come home, flop down to rest, and say about ten minutes worth of general "God-bless-us" prayers before taking on the day.

"I realized the time I spent with the Lord was like 'snack time' when 'banquet time' was what I really needed," she told me. "I decided to start praying first; then, if I had any time left, I would run."

During one of her first mornings of spending quality time with the Lord, he showed her a specific Scripture verse she could pray for her son. She paraphrased it: "Lord, may my son, like Jesus, increase in wisdom and stature and favor with God and man" (see Luke 2:52 KJV).

She didn't have to take Eugene in for the hormone shots because he began to grow. In the first three months after she started praying this way daily, he grew three inches! In the next three months, he grew three more. Some people may say that it was a natural growth spurt, but Eleanor is convinced God honored her prayer. She saw other evidence of answered prayer.

Her son's conduct grade on his report card went from a C minus to an A.

"Mom, my teacher likes me now, and I like her," he commented when she quizzed him about it.

"Eugene increased not only in stature and favor with his teacher, but in wisdom too as his other grades improved," Eleanor told me when I saw her months later. "Sometimes he laughs and says, 'Mom, I can't get away with anything anymore, because God always shows you when I've done something wrong.' But he's very interested to know what Scriptures I'm praying for him, and he is glad I'm praying so specifically.

"I still take time to run after my prayer time," she added, smiling. "But I find it more invigorating after coming directly from my prayer closet."

Praying Through Health Issues

When our children are ill, the same God who created their bodies has the power to heal them. We emphasize again that there is no guarantee that every prayer we utter for healing will result in a miracle. But we must remember this: We put our faith in God, not in the miracle of healing.

I (Quin) remember just a few years ago when my two-year-old granddaughter was desperately ill with double pneumonia. With her mom I stood over her hospital bed as day after day we laid our hands on her and asked God to heal her lungs and respiratory system. Later, with the help of medication and God's divine intervention, she was well enough to go home, though with machines to help her breathe more easily. We celebrated by having a party, complete with balloons!

Sometimes, in the winter, she is still plagued with bronchial infections, but her parents immediately get her on a machine to aid her breathing, and many people cover her in prayer.

Prayer of Faith

Maybe you have never prayed in faith for a physical healing. Here's a suggested prayer you can adapt as needed:

> Lord, I know that nothing is impossible with you. Jesus himself went about healing diseases and sicknesses when he lived on the earth. Your Word says that Jesus Christ is the same yesterday, today, and forever, so I know that you can heal today. Lord, please touch ___(name)___ with your healing power. I ask this in the name of Jesus, and I will be careful to give you all the glory. Amen.
>
> (See Luke 1:37, Matthew 4:23, and Hebrews 13:8.)

Dealing with the Unknown

Marilyn wrote us saying that when her oldest child was ten years old he suddenly developed a physical condition that left him unable to walk. She shares the story in her own words:

> Even after Paul was hospitalized and they did a spinal tap, the doctors found nothing concrete. We were dealing with a little bit of "x," "y," and "z," but it did not add up to any particular disease. It wasn't polio. It wasn't a brain tumor.
>
> Yes, I prayed. With all that was in me, I prayed!
>
> We had three small children at home, and I desperately tried to get professional help to stay with them. But it was a Thanksgiving holiday, and I could get no one, not even part-time. It was one of my darkest hours. A friend dealt treacherously against me and told others that I could afford help, so no one offered to babysit. It was a terrible time. I felt numb.

Dealing with a hospitalized child, plus three more at home, and a husband who was not emotionally supportive, was almost more than I could bear.

Paul spent two weeks in the hospital. Doctors would probe his muscles and make him move his legs—a very painful procedure. They let him watch on a television screen so he would understand what they were doing, but it didn't lessen his agony. Then came the recovery period at home. It began very slowly, but gradually, walking became normal for him. For years he suffered, and his cries in the night would awaken me. I would go to his room and wrap his legs in warm blankets and massage them. Since there was no clear diagnosis, there was no prescribed medical treatment. We were dealing with the unknown. We did the best we knew how, and eventually Paul stopped having the problem, but he was under the care of a neurologist for years.

Marilyn shares lessons she learned in her ordeal:

- to depend on God, even when her husband or friends offered little support

- to learn to pray faith-filled prayers based on the Bible

- to trust God for her son's complete healing, even when doctors could offer no explanation nor permanent treatment

These are the special promises which strengthened Marilyn during those difficult days:

He who comes to God must believe that He is, and that He is a rewarder of those who diligently seek Him (Hebrews 11:6 NKJV).

Hear my prayer, O LORD, and give ear to my cry; do not be silent at my tears (Psalm 39:12 NKJV).

Those who sow in tears shall reap in joy (Psalm 126:5 NKJV).

Finding Strength to Release Your Child

It is only natural for a Spirit-led mom to pray for her child's healing and full recovery, and to hold onto hope that God will intervene. Since the Scriptures encourage us to pray with faith for healing, we feel that's what every Spirit-led mom should do, even as she seeks medical help. Yet we must always keep our hearts open to God's overall plan.

Coming to the point of being able to release your child into God's hands, even if that means death, is probably one of the hardest decisions a parent ever has to make. Any mom who loses a child through illness or an accident must guard against feeling angry with God for not intervening.

Couldn't he have stopped something as evil as a drunk driver hitting and killing a child? Isn't his power greater than the disease that ravaged a child's body? Yes, of course God has the power to preserve life. With our human limitations, we will never be able to completely comprehend God's ways. His ways and his thoughts are so much higher than ours (see Isaiah 55:8-11). Because we live in a fallen world where people make wrong choices that affect others, tragedies sometimes occur in our children's lives. But God can comfort us, even when our prayers aren't answered as we had hoped.

One mom, still angry at God after her son's untimely death in an accident, went to a mountaintop to pray. "Why my son?" she shouted aloud to God through her tears. "He was wonderful! He had so much going for him."

As she quieted down, she sensed God's voice echoing back to her, *Why my Son?* The words of truth hit her like a hammer. God didn't intervene to prevent his own Son from dying on the cross, a horrible death that Jesus endured for her own forgiveness and redemption. As she sobbed, her healing and restoration began. She knew her son was with God's Son in heaven.[2]

This mom, and others like her, could take encouragement from Romans 14:8: "If we live, we live to the Lord; and if we die, we die to the Lord. So, whether we live or die, we belong to the Lord."

Prepare Them for Eternity

Here's a question most moms don't want to face: How do you choose between helping a child fight to live and relinquishing him to heaven? Some years ago I (Quin) posed that question to Fran, my prayer partner who is a nurse, physical therapist, and professional counselor.

"Talk to your child about his eternal being—that he is a spirit, he has a soul, and he lives in a body," she said. "The spirit within him will live on through eternity with the Lord, if he knows him. It's a mistake to allow our children to think this earthly life is all there is. We must teach them about heaven, and that living on earth is only the tiniest slice of life in preparation for life in heaven. Many times mothers have not led their little children to Jesus, thinking they were too young or that there was plenty of time later. It's never too early, or too late, for parents to do this."

She emphasized that moms should read aloud Scriptures which assure their children that there is no pain or sorrow where they are going, and that they will have a far better life in heaven than they did on earth.[3]

But of course, when face-to-face with the reality of death, only the Holy Spirit can truly prepare one to walk through such an ordeal. One of my (Ruthanne's) prayer partners shared with us her experience of finding God's peace and comfort in the midst of a very trying time.

How Could this Child We Love Leave Us?

When Vicki took her seven-year-old, Tim, for a checkup just after Christmas one year, she never dreamed he might be seriously ill. But what followed was a two-week blur of doctors and tests which finally resulted in a diagnosis of a rare form of childhood cancer, Berkett's Lymphoma. Vicki spent the next six weeks in a children's hospital watching her healthy little boy deteriorate before her eyes.

"Everyone we knew was praying and believing that God would surely heal him," she said. "But one night the Lord began to deal with me about my son. Who really was first in my life? Was I willing to give him up if God asked it of me? I thought of when God asked Abraham to sacrifice Isaac. After much wrestling with the question, the only answer I could give was yes. After all, Abraham didn't *really* have to give up Isaac, he just had to be willing to."

In mid-February Tim went into remission and was able to return to school, but he still needed regular blood checks. Over the next few weeks Vicki and her husband, John, took Tim to be prayed for by various ministers. But in late April, just before his eighth birthday, the cancer returned.

"The doctors didn't have many options available, because they had already used their best ammunition, chemotherapy, in the first round of treatment," Vicki said. "We were scared, yet still believing—but from then on Tim actually was beyond the help of treatment. His form of cancer was particularly fast-growing, and he was now unprotected by medicine. Prayer kept him going, but he wasn't getting well. Every night John and I had family prayer with Tim and his five-year-old sister, Alissa. At the end we had 'loving time' when we would all hug each other. Those are happy memories."

When they saw no improvement over the next two months, Vicki called several of her prayer partners, hoping for encouragement that her son would be healed. Her pastor's wife told her that while she was praying for Tim, she saw in her mind's eye their whole family kneeling before a bright, radiating light that she felt represented the Lord. Then she saw Tim slowly move away from his parents and sister into the light of God's presence.

Hearing this devastated Vicki. How could this child they loved so much leave them? Their Christian friends and family rallied to offer comfort and support. One of the group shared with them about the "prayer of relinquishment" presented in Catherine Marshall's book, *Adventures in Prayer*. That night they read the chapter, even as Tim's pain and suffering intensified.

"John and I knelt beside our bed and gave him to the Lord," Vicki said. "It truly was a dying of our will and submission to God's will—a very hard thing to do. The next morning, Tim's discomfort was eased, and he needed no more pain medicine from that day forward. The Lord spoke to me that Tim would be more at home with him in heaven than he had been on earth. Knowing we would lose Tim broke my heart, yet I had a sense of God's peace, also knowing our son would be safe in the Father's arms."

A friend had made a tape recording of her worship songs for Tim, and that was all he wanted to listen to during his last few days. He would lie peacefully, eyes closed, listening to the music—almost as if he were in heaven already. On the fifth day after Vicki and John prayed the prayer of relinquishment, Vicki walked into Tim's room just in time to see him breathe his final breath. At last he was with the Lord.

"God showed himself strong in so many ways," she said. "After we knew he was dying, the Lord gave us time to make plans. We had a small graveside ceremony in the morning, followed by a large memorial service that evening, complete with a full choir singing 'The Hallelujah Chorus.'

"A few weeks later, as I was looking through the Bible storybook which I had read to Tim, God comforted me through some of the illustrations. There was a drawing of the young biblical

Timothy, looking very much like our Tim, sitting on his grand-mother's lap and listening to her read the Scriptures. That was the way Tim had been with us. It was a precious moment.

"Then I was drawn to the illustration of the boy Samuel. The child in the drawing had the same physical characteristics as our Tim. In this picture an alert, smiling 'Tim' was on his pallet with his ear cocked to hear the voice of God. *That is how he is now*, the Lord seemed to say to me.

"We had prayed for a son just as Samuel's mother, Hannah, had done. When God answered Hannah's prayer, she kept her vow to God and took her son to live and serve in the Lord's house. I suddenly realized how our Tim, like Samuel, was now living and serving our Lord in his house. That gave me great comfort."

The transition to life without Tim was painful, but Vicki has sweet memories of this special child who was God's gift to their family for a few short years. And she knows they will be together in heaven some day.

"We parents must always remember that our children are first and last the Lord's," she wrote. "He created them, died for them, and has prepared a life and a place for them. We are not their Savior, only their nurturers and trainers. Even if they live a long life, they are under our roof for a very short time. We should make the most of those precious days."

Finding God in the Midst of Trauma

Sometimes moms draw closer to the Lord when one of their children experiences illness or physical trauma. Certainly Vicki came to know God in a deeper way than ever before as she experienced the loss of her son, and she is able to offer comfort to other moms who suffer such a loss. In the case of Joan, her son's crisis led her from being a nominal church member to truly becoming a Spirit-led mom.

After resisting the idea of letting her ten-year-old son, Alex, play peewee football for fear he'd get hurt, she finally relented and let him sign up. But just moments after her son and his friend left her backyard to go to their first practice session, someone ran to tell her that Alex had been hit by a car as they were crossing the street.

"When I got there it was a gruesome scene," Joan remembers. "Alex had flown over the hood of the car and was lying in the street, crying. Blood was splattered all over him and the femur in his left leg was poking through the skin. As I cradled him in my lap I began reciting the twenty-third psalm—it was the only thing I could think of to do. At the hospital Alex underwent three hours of surgery for what doctors called 'catastrophic injuries,' and then they put him in a body cast."

When Joan arrived home that night, she collapsed in a crying jag, feeling completely weak and helpless. She had kept her feelings under control while she was with Alex, but now, alone at home, she just lost it.

"Still crying, I picked up my Bible and tried to read some psalms," she said. "But they seemed so dry and lifeless. Suddenly I realized that though I was a religious woman, I didn't have a relationship with the God whom David the psalmist knew so well. At that moment I began my search to truly find him, knowing I would need to be empowered with his strength and wisdom for what lay ahead of us."

Three weeks after his surgery, Alex came home to a hospital bed set up in their dining room for seven long months of recuperation. Through an intercom hooked up to his classroom, he kept up with his studies. He graduated from a body cast to leg casts and underwent months of physical therapy to learn to walk again. His mother was his constant companion and nurse.

One autumn night as Joan was listening to a Billy Graham crusade sermon on television, she quietly said yes to Christ's lordship in her life. Shortly afterward, she began to read books about the power of the Holy Spirit. She longed to know that kind of power—to live in total trust and dependence on God and to believe him even for miracles.

Then, out of curiosity, she accepted an invitation to attend a Wednesday night service at a church of a denomination different from her own. "I was thrilled with the lively singing and the preaching that exalted Christ," she said. "When the pastor invited those who wanted prayer to receive the Holy Spirit to come forward, I was among the first to go. As the pastor prayed, I was overwhelmed with God's presence, peace, and power. At last I knew the joy of a personal relationship with him."

A short time later, on Easter weekend, Joan found herself crying uncontrollably, but for no apparent reason. "As I questioned what this could mean, I had a mental image of myself kneeling in the street beside my son after he'd been hit by a car. It seemed that I was feeling the grief and heartache of Father God over what his Son endured on the cross for my sins. I stopped and thanked him over and over for his death on the cross for me and my family.

"The Lord was so kind and merciful to use my son's accident to draw me to himself," she said. "Alex and I will never forget the exact date of his accident. We send notes to one another around that time every year, thanking God for sparing his life."

Right now, you may think back to a time when God moved miraculously in your life or the life of one of your children. Maybe you will you want to audibly thank him for his protection, for a gift of healing, or for whatever miracle you can recall.

Prayer

Lord, I do thank you for all the times you came to my aid in difficult situations when someone in my family needed a healing touch from you. I will never take for granted your divine protection and intervention. I am so grateful I can continue to trust you in each circumstance I face in the future. Amen.

Scriptures for Meditation

"Heal me, O LORD, and I will be healed; save me and I will be saved, for you are the one I praise" (Jeremiah 17:14).

"Now Lord...enable your servants to speak your word with great boldness. Stretch out your hand to heal and perform miraculous signs and wonders through the name of your holy servant Jesus" (Acts 4:29-30).

"You know what has happened throughout Judea...how God anointed Jesus of Nazareth with the Holy Spirit and power, and how he went around doing good and healing all who were under the power of the devil, because God was with him" (Acts 10:37-38).

"Dear children, let us not love with words or tongue but with actions and in truth. This then is how we know that we belong to the truth, and how we set our hearts at rest in his presence whenever our hearts condemn us. For God is greater than our hearts, and he knows everything" (1 John 3:18-19).

"I pray that you may enjoy good health and that all may go well with you, even as your soul is getting along well" (3 John 2).

10
Power to Mentor Your Children
Building a Life of Faith

*Only be careful, and watch yourselves closely so that you
do not forget the things your eyes have seen or let them slip
from your heart as long as you live. Teach them to your
children and to their children after them.*
—DEUTERONOMY 4:9

*Children are our investment in the future. They will bear the
imprint of our mothering throughout their lives. As mothers, we
teach our children all the values we believe must be passed on to the
next generation: love, faithfulness, trust, obedience, respect,
honesty, loyalty...When we mother well, we teach our children to
embrace the moral obligations that build solid relationships, healthy
marriages, and secure families. Oh, what a sacred gift it is when
a woman receives the title Mother! There is no higher calling.[1]*
—JANI ORTLUND

Perhaps the single most important role for the Christian
mother is that of raising her child in the fear and
knowledge of the Lord. How can she best fulfill this
responsibility?

You may have heard the expression, "I'd rather see a sermon
than hear one any day." Often our "modeling" of Christian
behavior before our children is the primary way we unconsciously
mentor them.

Gloria Gaither once wrote:

> Sometimes we adults associate learning [only] with books...But when the books are closed and the lessons are over, children go on learning. No knobs turn off their little minds...They go on learning, watching me, seeing how I handle problems, sensing my unguarded reactions, picking up the "vibes" of our home.[2]

Teaching by Example

A story shared by Elisa Morgan, president of MOPS (Mothers of Preschoolers) illustrates how our reactions to everyday problems can impact our children.

One day her daughter Eva lost her orthodontic retainer when she left it on her school lunchroom tray. As any mother would, Elisa wanted her daughter to learn to be responsible. When Eva called to say, "Mom, you are going to kill me..." and proceeded to tell her what had happened, Elisa headed for the school.

On the way a voice seemed to warn her, *Elisa, the way you respond to your daughter when she's nine and has lost her retainer is the way she will assume you'll respond to her when she is sixteen and has made a more serious mistake.*

Upon reaching the school, Elisa helped her daughter search everywhere for the retainer—even to climbing onto a wobbly chair to hang over the side of the school's trash dumpster. She gingerly picked through plastic bags and peanut butter sandwiches soaked in chocolate milk. Plenty upset over her carelessness, Eva was crying as she, too, searched through the soggy garbage. But the retainer was nowhere to be found.

Remembering the earlier warning, which obviously was from God, Elisa realized she had to forgive Eva. *How I respond today is how she will assume I'll respond in the future,* she reminded herself. *What she finds in me is much of what she'll expect to find in God.*

Eva had said she was sorry, and it was clear that she meant it. Perhaps that was the key. Abandoning the search, Elisa got off the chair and took Eva in her arms, assuring her that she was forgiven. She called the orthodontist for an appointment to get a new retainer and asked her daughter to contribute $25 from her savings account toward the cost of it.

"Then I let go of it," she says, "the way God lets go of all the mistakes I make." She recalled 1 John 1:9: "If we confess our sins, he is faithful and just and will forgive us our sins and purify us from all unrighteousness." Because the child confessed her sin of carelessness and was truly remorseful, the mom forgave her just as God would do.[3]

Who knows how often Eva will recall that experience and draw on the same power of Christ to enable her to forgive someone? Her mom was not only modeling how to forgive, but also how to respond without anger.

Remember how Eva began her phone call to her mom with "You are going to kill me..."? Well, Eva's mom didn't overreact to her carelessness with harsh condemnation and punishment. However, to stress the importance of responsibility, Elisa did ask Eva to help pay for the lost item. It was an appropriate response. One day they'll probably sit down together and laugh over their experience of searching in vain through stinky garbage.

When I (Quin) read Elisa's story, I thought of times when I had reacted wrongly to something one of my children had done that aggravated me greatly. And I was convicted!

Passing on Your Ideals

Each Spirit-led mom must determine which ideals she feels God wants her to hand on to her children. Here are a few basics:

   ❧ Be a godly example to them in the way you allow the Holy Spirit to help you in dealing with disappointments and hard situations in your own life. They will remember your actions more clearly than your words.

❧ Help them understand the importance of choosing friends who will have a positive influence on them, not a negative one. Always be willing to offer hospitality to their friends.

❧ Continually encourage them to talk about their own feelings (anger, hurt, disappointment), but never express shock at something they say. Pray with them to demonstrate how they can talk to God about these things and ask for his help. Give them guidelines for handling their emotions in a sensible, healthy way as they discuss their issues with you.

❧ Teach them to be kind to people from different cultural, ethnic, and social backgrounds, yet warn them of the dangers of associating with those whose morals are contrary to what the Bible teaches.

❧ Help them learn how to interpret the news on television and in the newspaper in light of God's Word. Be open to discussing with your children both sides of controversial issues.

Helping Her Children "See" God

Doris, a single working mom with two kids in elementary school and two in high school, is always looking for ways to instill spiritual values in her children. She has flexible office hours, and sometimes brings work home with her, but for now their needs come first.

"I'm glad I learned how to have intimate times of prayer with God before I became a single mom," she said. "I find myself praying more for God's grace, and for me to have wisdom about many decisions concerning the children. I want them to learn to

depend on the Lord, so as a family we stop and pray more, especially since their daddy left. It's reassuring to know that God is
always there to help me through each situation that comes up."

Doris reminisced about the time when her two-year-old,
Anna, scooted into the kitchen on her little bike one day and
announced, "Mommy, I want to see God!"

She knelt down beside Anna and said, "Well, honey, you
can't really see God like you see Mommy right now. But we know
he's there, because—"

That wasn't the answer she wanted. "No, Mommy. I want to
hold God," she insisted.

Doris pulled her toddler into her lap, laid her head against
hers, and cried for a minute. "The truth is, I want to hold God
too," she said, looking back on the experience. "In moments
Anna hopped down, got back on her little bike, and scooted
down the hall. But I was left with an eternal memory—and a
desire to keep alive in the hearts of all my children that innocent
hunger for God."

Doris now has to do at night what she used to do during the
day—wash clothes, clean house, pay bills, and cook meals to
store in the freezer. But these late nights are special prayer times
for her.

"Praying is a priority for me and has been for years," she said.
"Also, togetherness is a word we live by at our house these days.
On Monday nights I lead a family devotional for all four kids.
When I need to work in the yard, we all work there together. If
I clean a closet, they help. They have their own chores, but we
do as many things together as possible. Discipline has been a
problem, but when I have to discipline them, we sit down and
talk about why, so they understand very clearly that Mom is not
a 'meanie.'"

This is a prayer Doris often prays:

> Come, Holy Spirit, and show me how to meet the
> needs of each of my children today. Walk with me

through their ups and downs. Let me experience God's presence so that when I touch them, they, too, will feel his love and embrace. Let me be your hands extended to them. Open their spiritual eyes so they can see you all around them—in people, in the earth and sky, in church, in school—wherever they go. Draw all of us closer to you and to one another. In Jesus' name, amen.

Encouraging Children to Worship

Darlene, who has five- and eight-year-old sons, puts a high priority on seeking to bring the presence of God into her home in such a way that her children can actually feel it. "I play worship music on a regular basis and encourage my children to dance, play drums or guitars, or participate in whatever way they can," she said. "We even dance together at times!"

When they were toddlers, Darlene trained them to be quiet and watch as Mommy worshiped Jesus when the more intimate, worshipful songs were played.

"It can take a lot of concentration to try to enter the presence of God with a child crawling all over you," she said. "But the value in those moments is priceless, as your children learn not only that God always comes first in life, but that they can enter into his presence. Allowing your children to enter into your private life with God gives them a picture of the intimacy of a relationship with Christ that they will never fully understand just attending church. They must see it in action."

Darlene has devotions with her boys and allows them to highlight in their Bibles the verses they read. As she teaches on the chosen verses, they sometimes take notes or draw pictures in their notebooks about what they learn. They always close with prayer, and Darlene has the boys lay hands on each other, and on her, as they pray.

"Raising godly children today demands much more than just living a godly life yourself and hoping they pick it up by osmosis," she said. "One of the most profound ideas the Holy Spirit ever laid on my heart for these quiet times was to use the actual Word of God, but put it in toddler language. Instead of using children's devotional books, we use the Bible, but I make the language easier for them to understand—sometimes with hand and body motions. When we memorized the Ten Commandments, this is the way I worded it for them:

1. Put God first.

2. Don't bow down to any other gods.

3. Don't use God's name for bad things.

4. Go to church and think about God on Sundays.

5. Obey your Mommy and Daddy.

6. Don't hurt anybody.

7. Mommies and Daddies have to love each other.

8. Don't take things that aren't yours.

9. Never tell a lie.

10. Be happy with what you already have.

Darlene feels it's important to look for indicators of what your children's spiritual gifts are and encourage their expression.

"I firmly believe God speaks through children on a regular basis, but most of us just aren't paying attention," she said. "My oldest son has always shown signs of prophetic gifts, and I learned early on to pay attention to his words and not brush him aside. Many times he would bring up someone's name and ask to pray for him or her, and then I would later discover that person really had needed prayer at that precise moment. Watch for these signs of spiritual gifts in your children, and don't despise their ability to move in the Spirit simply because of their youth. They are often more in touch with the pure presence of God than we are."

Give Them a Prayer Legacy

One of the most powerful legacies we can leave our children is a prayer heritage. If we want them to learn to pray, they must hear us pray. There is no greater demonstration of God's power to our children than when they see us—their parents—receive answers to prayer.

From the time my son, Bradley, was able to talk, I (Ruthanne) always prayed with him at bedtime and encouraged him to pray. When he was small he would voluntarily pray for a school class-mate or for someone being loaded into an ambulance when we passed the scene of an accident. But in his teenage years he went through a period of seeming to resent my suggestion that we pray about a problem.

One afternoon when Bradley came home from high school he asked me what I'd been doing that day. "Some of my prayer part-ners came over for lunch and we had a prayer meeting," I replied.

"I bet you all prayed for me, didn't you?" he asked sarcastically.

"Yes, we did. We prayed about lots of things," I said.

"Well, I don't like the idea of people I don't even know praying for me," he answered as he stormed out of the kitchen.

I just ignored his comment and continued preparing dinner while thinking to myself, *One of these days you're going to appre-ciate having people pray for you.*

During that turbulent school year Bradley had applied to his university of choice, and we had prayed he would be accepted. When that didn't happen, he was angry. "All your prayers just aren't going to cut it, Mom," he said. I didn't argue; I just kept praying. And God answered another way (see the full story in chapter 6).

Now, many years later, he calls home to ask for prayer on a regular basis—not only for his own problems, but also for his friends. And he often makes a point of asking me to call my prayer partners with his prayer requests. Several times he has asked me to send one of our books on prayer to a friend who was struggling.

Don't be deterred if your child goes through a period when he or she resists your prayers. Just continue to set the example in prayer, and one day you will reap the benefits.

Years ago a missionary to Africa taught me (Quin) a short prayer which I taught to my children and then to my grandchildren. Though I don't know the author, it's a delightful prayer to begin the day:

> Good morning, God.
> This is your day.
> I am your child.
> Show me your way today. Amen.

We can pass on to our children the model of our own personal prayer lives, after which they can establish their own. I have watched my adult children almost outdistance me in prayer in recent years. Since becoming parents themselves, they've learned the importance of praying earnestly for the little ones God has entrusted to them.

I am often amused when I see my six-year-old granddaughter, Victoria, pacing up and down in my bedroom "talking to Jesus" in a loud voice with her hands on her hips, just as her mom does. It's never too early for youngsters to learn to pray. In fact, when they hear us pray, they just seem to want to imitate us.

A mom once told me she tried to shoo her young daughter out of her bedroom while she prayed, but the Lord stopped her. *She has the same Holy Spirit you do,* God seemed to say. *Let her join in your prayer meeting as you help her develop her prayer life.* Today that daughter is a mom who includes her own little girl in her private prayer times.

Esther Ilnisky, who has organized an international network of praying children, believes godly children are the most untapped resource of prayer, both in the home and in the church worldwide. She says, "If children are not given a credible place in the spiritual life of families and churches today, it is possible they will not be prepared to be strong members and leaders in the families and churches of tomorrow."[4]

Teaching Children to Love the Word of God

Besides teaching their children to pray, Spirit-led moms also desire to impart to them a love for God's Word. Our friend Rachel Burchfield and her husband operate a Bible school and summer camp ministry in Texas that impacts the lives of thousands of young people every year. Naturally, she believes in establishing Bible-reading habits in children from the time they are young.

When one of her sons, at age seven, started fussing about reading the Bible every night, Rachel was concerned that if she forced him, he would resent the Word of God. She didn't want to be a nagging mother. She prayed about the matter and was surprised by the Lord's response.

Don't you remind (nag) him each night to brush his teeth whether he wants to or not? the Lord said. *How much more important is his spiritual growth?*

That settled it for Rachel. "From that night on, I first helped him read and, if I had any energy left, we pursued the conquest of brushing his teeth," she wrote. "Habits will make or break your children...God's Word in children's hearts is enough to save them, and to keep them holy until heaven."

She proposes three guidelines to help children with Bible-reading:

1. Keep it short. It's important to adjust the reading time to the child's attention span—which usually matches his age. A seven-year-old should be challenged to read for

seven minutes. She suggests having the children focus on reading the words of Jesus and exciting Bible stories.

2. Keep it repetitive. She makes "courage cards" for her three children each week—which are neon-colored index cards with several Scriptures printed on them. She keeps them in the car, and each day during the ten-minute ride to school, the children read aloud the verses on the cards. By Friday they have most of the Scriptures for that week memorized.

3. Keep it personal. She suggests getting an age-appropriate Bible for each child with his or her name engraved on it and teaching the child to treat it with respect. Encourage each child to read parts of the Bible that match his or her interest. Boys often enjoy reading about Jehoshaphat's miracle battle (2 Chronicles 20) or Gideon's army (Judges 6 and 7). If your child is a musician, encourage her to read the Psalms and then make up her own songs to the Lord.[5]

Ruth Bell Graham offers this challenge to potential mentors:

> Like wind surfing, the Christian life is simple but not easy. And we are not born into God's family fully grown, although at times we treat baby Christians as if they should have been.
>
> We who are older in the Christian walk and those who, through experience, have earned the status of instructor should be quick to encourage, quick to help the one who has fallen. We who have not yet mastered the art of Christian living need to keep carefully studying our Book of Instructions, listening attentively when our Instructor speaks, and promptly following His instructions.[6]

What Is a Mentor?

"What exactly is a mentor?" you may be asking. It's a mom like you who passes down to a child with less understanding her knowledge and insight. This transfer of wisdom, based on one's life experience, happens one-on-one over time, rather than through formal classroom-type methods. A good definition of a mentor is *someone who encourages and equips another for excellence*.

A mom who wants to mentor her children will teach them manners, graciousness, and practical ways to deal with life's problems. They will learn from her example that home is a place for comfort, healing, friendship, nourishment, rest, and encouragement. But even more important, Spirit-led moms will instill in them godly principles.

"I want to be spiritual without being rigorously religious," one mom told us. "I don't want to impose 'you shall not do this' rules in such a strict, nonnegotiable way that my kids run from God instead of running to him. In some instances they have the freedom to come to me and state their case. I may tell them, 'Let's both go pray about that and then come back and see what God has spoken to us individually.' It keeps us open to talk, but it also teaches them to hear from God and to trust that I am doing what is best for them because I listen to him too. But the bottom line is that I'm the parent, I'm responsible for them, and I have the final say-so."

We see in New Testament times that Lois instilled spiritual truths in her daughter Eunice, who had a son named Timothy. Together the grandmother and mother had a godly influence on this young evangelist who would be one of the apostle Paul's successors (see 2 Timothy 1:5).

Never forget that children have a tender place in the heart of the Lord. Once when his disciples argued over who would be the greatest, Jesus stood a little child beside him and said, "whoever welcomes this little child in my name welcomes me; and whoever welcomes me welcomes the one who sent me. For he who is least among you all—he is the greatest" (Luke 9:48).

Children who catch on quickly to spiritual truths sometimes surprise us by their boldness. When my (Ruthanne's) 13-year-old granddaughter, Rachel, was attending a music camp one summer, she was dismayed that some of the girls in the dorm used foul language. As the week began, the counselor asked the girls to make suggestions as to what the dorm rules should be. This was not a Christian camp, but Rachel spoke up and said she thought there should be no swearing allowed. Only one other girl agreed, but the counselor said it was a good idea, and "no swearing" became a rule.

After this, every time one of the girls would use curse words in her hearing, Rachel would point her finger at the offender in a teasing manner and say, "Bad word! Bad word! Bad word!" It didn't make her very popular with some of her dormmates, but she stood her ground. Eventually she saw the profanity level drop drastically. Her mom was so proud of her when Rachel returned home and shared the experience with her family.

Often a young mom needs the influence of an older woman to give her answers to those perplexing questions that arise during child-rearing years. If her own mother lives hundreds of miles away, she can seek out a godly woman whom she would like to emulate—usually finding such a person right in her own church or neighborhood. The older woman's knowledge, wisdom, and expertise is something she can draw on, put into practice, and eventually pass on to her children, as we see in Pam's experience.

God Can Lead You to a Mentor

For the past seven years, Pam, a working mom, has been stopping by her friend JoAnne's house every morning on the way to work to pray with her for half an hour. After hearing this seasoned intercessor pray aloud at a National Day of Prayer gathering, Pam knew she wanted to learn from this woman. When she sought her out and asked if she could meet with her regularly to pray, JoAnne agreed.

"I have grown in my relationship with the Lord so much as JoAnne has mentored me and taught me," Pam reported. "I had little knowledge of the Bible to begin with, but you can learn the Scriptures just from hearing JoAnne pray. I look to her as a mom, and my three sons look to her as a grandma and ask for her prayers. One of my sons, who was a great prayer challenge in his younger years, now serves as a missionary in Africa. The spiritual progress my boys have made is largely because of my determination to get up early each morning to go pray with JoAnne—and it's time well spent. We pray for our community, state, nation, leaders—even the schools my kids attend."

Perhaps you don't have a mentor because you haven't considered all the possibilities. But, like Pam, if you begin to open your eyes and ears, God will lead you to one who can teach you the spiritual lessons you need to learn.

Pass On the Vision for Mentoring

We asked a pastor's wife of a large metropolitan church who mentors many young moms what are the most important things she shares with them. She told us:

> I teach them what I have learned from my own life: to love your child unconditionally, to learn the power of prayer, to find a compatible prayer partner, and to stop having false expectations that can lead you to great disappointments. You need to enjoy the present moment with your child. Not what he could be, not what he should be, not what he ought to be—but the jewel that child is at the moment. I cry with women going through hard situations because I've been there myself. But I can also say I have learned

not to let circumstances turn my heart away from God. Sometimes when we think we are facing the most impossible situation, later on we will see it from a different perspective and be able to testify about the goodness of God in it.

Mentoring our children means passing on to them our values and beliefs that are important and invaluable. We open new windows for them. We express our pride and confidence in them. We invest in their future. They, in turn, can be led by the Holy Spirit to pass these treasures to the next generation.

Sarah is a young teenager who shared with us her excitement about The Call—a spiritual event where thousands of youth have met in numerous cities across the country to worship, fast, and pray for the destiny of their generation. She and her younger sister, along with their parents, have participated in five of these events thus far.

"The last one I attended was about generational reconciliation, and it was life-changing for me," Sarah said. "It was so powerful to see kids my age turning toward their fathers and mothers, and to see the parents turning their hearts to their children. We really need our parents' guidance in our lives. If we will wholeheartedly grab onto this idea of reconciliation between the older and younger generations, I believe we'll see God move as he has never moved before."

One of the Scriptures highlighted at the latest gathering Sarah attended was Malachi 4:6: "He will turn the hearts of the fathers to their children, and the hearts of the children to their fathers."

This statement—the last verse in the Old Testament—is like a bridge leading us into the future with the hope of healing between the generations. As Spirit-led moms, we have a glorious opportunity to instruct our children in the ways of the Holy Spirit and to inspire them to follow his leading with no holds barred.

What an inheritance we have to pass on to them!

Prayer

Almighty God, help me to mentor my children in your ways so they will fulfill your purpose for them here on earth. Show me ways to teach them both practical and spiritual truths. Give me creative ideas, patience, and great wisdom to fulfill my role as a mom. Lord, when I need some hands-on help in my child-rearing duties, lead me to an older woman I can trust for advice or mentoring. Thank you, precious Lord. Amen.

Scriptures for Meditation

"These commandments that I give you today are to be upon your hearts. Impress them on your children. Talk about them when you sit at home and when you walk along the road, when you lie down and when you get up" (Deuteronomy 6:6-7).

"Know therefore that the LORD your God is God; he is the faithful God, keeping his covenant of love to a thousand generations of those who love him and keep his commands" (Deuteronomy 7:9).

"We will tell the next generation the praiseworthy deeds of the LORD, his power, and the wonders he has done" (Psalm 78:4).

"She opens her mouth in skillful and godly Wisdom, and on her tongue is the law of kindness [giving counsel and instruction]" (Proverbs 31:26 AMP).

"Go therefore and make disciples…teaching them to observe all that I commanded you; and lo, I am with you always, even to the end of the age" (Matthew 28:19-20 NASB).

"The goal of our instruction is love from a pure heart and a good conscience and a sincere faith" (1 Timothy 1:5 NASB).

11
Power to Enjoy Life as a Family
Embracing the Joy of the Lord

May the LORD give you increase more and more, you and
your children. May you be blessed by the LORD,
who made heaven and earth.
—PSALM 115:14-15 NKJV

The family is the place where the deep understanding that people
are significant, important, worthwhile, with a purpose in life,
should be learned at an early age. The family is the place where
children should learn that human beings have been made in
the image of God and are therefore very special in the universe.[1]
—EDITH SCHAEFFER

God's world is filled with good things for a mom and her children to enjoy together. As her offspring grow up, leave the nest, and then have families of their own, Mom and memories of home often form the linchpin that helps keep everyone connected.

We hope to help you find family joy and the delight of sharing it with your children through all the phases of their lives. Maybe some of the ideas and stories presented here will inspire creative ideas of your own.

Some years ago I (Quin) received a letter from my friend Pat King, the mother of ten children. She wrote about her experience of dropping in to visit another mom:

One morning I stopped in to see my friend Julie, who had four children under the age of five. Remembering my own days of little children, my heart often went out to her. As I let myself in the back door and heard the sounds of laughter coming from the children's bedroom, I peered in the doorway. There was Julie and her three oldest children sitting in a circle on the floor with a dishtowel spread out in the middle as a tablecloth. The baby watched from his bed as Julie poured water into the children's teacups and divided up some raisins and graham crackers. "Now, Mrs. Jones," she asked her three-year-old, "would you like milk or sugar in your tea?"

Julie's smile acknowledged me in the doorway, but she went on with her tea party as if she were entertaining the most important people in the world. I watched for a few moments and then slipped out the back door and drove home.[2]

Here was a mom who knew that spending fun time with her children was a higher priority than visiting with an adult friend—something she could always do at a future time. Years after I received that note from Pat, one of my daughters gave me a plaque with this inscription. I hung it in my bedroom as a constant reminder of where to place my priorities:

> One hundred years
> from now it will not matter
> what your bank account held,
> the sort of home you lived in,
> or the kind of car you drove.
> But the world may be a
> different place because you
> were important in the life
> of a child.
> —AUTHOR UNKNOWN

Important in the life of a child—yes, that's what I want to be.

Finding Ways to Have Fun

To help children develop good self-esteem, moms often need to experiment to discover the activities which most interest them and then encourage them to develop a potential talent. For instance, one mom whose daughter had a noticeable artistic bent provided art lessons for her when she turned eight. The whole family began to visit art museums and became somewhat involved in her interest. They took short trips to places with beautiful scenery for the budding artist to sketch or paint while other family members went water skiing or just enjoyed the outdoors.

Other possible options for family activities are taking nature walks, going on trips to libraries, rock collecting, swimming, camping, picnicking, biking, skating, playing tennis or other sports, playing board games, doing crafts together, and, of course, reading together.

When my (Ruthanne's) family lived just outside Brussels, Belgium, for almost four years, we enjoyed excursions to the coast to ride the paddle boats, trips to the historic Waterloo Battlefield (which was only a few miles from our house), tours through museums, castles, and old churches, and visits to flea markets while munching hot Belgian waffles bought from street vendors.

Recently I came across a unique brass-and-glass candy dish I had purchased on one of those family flea market excursions more than 30 years ago. I polished it up, filled it with gummy bears—our son's favorite boyhood candy—and sent it to Bradley for his birthday. He called to thank me and said it brought back memories of his childhood when that dish sat on the coffee table in our old Belgian house. He reminisced about looking inside it to find the surprise I would leave for him when he had to spend an evening with a babysitter, and he remembered the year he found an Easter egg at the bottom of the dish. Of course that gift meant a lot more to him than an expensive shirt or sweater would have.

Because we were teaching at a Bible school and living on a missionary budget, we had to find economical ways to enjoy our leisure time. Often we would drive to southern Holland to a huge outdoor market where we could buy household goods and clothing for the kids far more reasonably than in Belgium. We would pack a picnic lunch and make it a fun outing on a Saturday.

I don't remember praying specifically to ask for guidance on how we could have fun as a family. But I believe the Holy Spirit gave John and me some creative ideas for activities that our kids really enjoyed and still remember.

Exploring and Learning Together

Our (Quin's) family planned camping trips as a means to ensure some quality family time. However, we also used these trips to teach history lessons. By the time our youngest was in first grade, we had explored more than 35 states, sleeping in the pop-up camper we pulled behind our station wagon. With history books in hand we set out to show our kids Plymouth Rock, Jamestown, Washington, D.C., native American reservations, caverns, the dells of Wisconsin, the gravesites of presidents, the home of Mark Twain, the mountains and deserts throughout the West, and many other historic landmarks. We visited space sites in three states and spent a week in Key West letting our children fish and explore.

We also enjoyed going camping with friends. Some weekends it was not unusual for as many as 40 of us from our church to camp together and have a Sunday morning worship service out in the open. The kids who accompanied their parents on our outings loved building forts, going canoeing or fishing, and taking nighttime guided cruises through Florida's nature parks.

Naturally, a family's activities are influenced by your geographic location, and the activities will change as the children grow older. What you did together when they were young will not always work when they are teens. When our three became teenagers and were no longer interested in camping, we sold our camper. We always tried, however, to keep the family involved in some type of common recreation.

Carving out time for fun with the family can be especially hard for moms who work outside the home. Finding a healthy balance is often a constant struggle. I (Quin) understand this stress because I wrote for a daily newspaper when my children were growing up. My boss allowed me flexible hours so that I was home with my children after school hours and during holidays and summers. It was difficult to keep the house cleaned, clothes washed, help with homework, and find some time to have fun with the kids after I got in from work. But making the children my priority was worth the effort.

Today I have a daughter and daughter-in-love whose "at home" businesses allow them to be there when their kids get in from school. However, another daughter must work full-time and has to put her son in child care both before and after school. To compensate, my husband and I often take him on picnics, skating, and to nearby parks to play ball.

Sometimes all six cousins, ages two to eight, get together at our house for a softball game or sledding down the hill when the snow is deep. But their annual event is the Cousins' Christmas Party when they dress up, exchange gifts, enjoy refreshments, and play games planned just for them. We rotate houses for this occasion.

Overcoming a Limited Budget

"Every night our family of four eats together in the dining room where there is no television, and we have a lot of laughter and sharing," says DeeAnn, mother of two children ages ten and twelve. "After a relaxed family fun time, my children are much more willing to talk about their concerns and issues."

When the children were younger, DeeAnn would place a jar in the middle of the dinner table with family history questions and fun facts written on slips of paper. After they finished eating, the children took turns drawing a question and reading it aloud. "This was a good way for us to teach them about their family heritage and to stimulate good conversation about topics we wanted them to address," she explains. "Sometimes they would consult a dictionary, encyclopedia, or Bible to find the answer to a 'fact question.' "

On Sunday afternoons they often play family board games for three-hour stretches. In the summer they go biking, hiking, or camping. During car trips they enjoy playing guessing games; then they stop off at roadside parks for a game of Frisbee. Because all the family enjoys music, they have sing-alongs while Dad plays guitar and 12-year-old Jules plays drums. Friday nights are movie nights—either at home or in a theater. Visits with grandparents who live nearby also provide rich times for the children to enjoy intergenerational sharing. They take turns having a sleepover at Grandma and Grandpa's house.

"We see good fruit in our children because of the hours we have invested in family time," DeeAnn says. "They are well rooted in the foundation of God. Sometimes it just seems natural to ask the kids, 'How did Jesus show himself to you today?' "

Reading is one valuable but inexpensive way to connect with your children. Jayleen, the mother of three girls and two boys, ages three to eleven, feels that reading to her children is a high priority. Just before bedtime they gather in the living room for her to read from a series of books about the adventures and values of a little boy's family who moved to a Colorado ranch in the early 1900s. They never tire of hearing the stories over and over.

The four older children are taking violin lessons. When they found out their teacher is paid to play in the city's orchestra while doing something she really enjoys, they were even more motivated to practice. Then one Sunday when a young woman played a violin solo in church, they told their mom they wanted to be able to worship God like that with their instruments. Jayleen displays great interest in their music and encourages them as she drives them to and from their lessons.

Seeing the country on a limited budget was another challenge she took on last year. Jayleen and her sister packed their kids and belongings into a van—eight kids in all—and started out on a three-week, 5000-mile journey to see historical sights across the eastern states. When they got to New York, Jayleen's husband met them, and they joined thousands of other Christians at The Call, a gathering of youth and parents who met to pray for our nation.

"After the kids had been penned up in the car all day, they needed to exercise and play, so we would stop at campsites and set up the tent. They could run, swim, play Ping-Pong, or participate in other recreational activities available on the grounds. Occasionally we stayed with friends, letting the children snuggle up in sleeping bags on the floor. We had a very limited budget for a trip like this, but we did it."

Another fun time for her children is spending a night at Grandma's (Oma's). She only takes one child at a time to make each one feel special. Using a jar of pennies, Grandma has come up with her own method of teaching the children math along with the principle of tithing. They come home with pennies for church and pennies for themselves. Jayleen feels this hands-on touch from her mother is very important to her kids, as they haven't always lived close to her, and Grandma recently lost her husband. "We need her and she needs us," she said.

Fun, Feasts, and Festivals

Birthdays, anniversaries, awards, or even the slightest reason provide families opportunities to celebrate and encourage one another. Some families just naturally seem to adopt significant days they celebrate, while others rarely commemorate special events. What a pity! We (the Sherrers) once had a college student living with us who had never had a birthday party. Did we ever throw him one! Years later he was still writing to thank us.

Have you considered starting a new tradition with your children? Finding a way to observe something you have never done before? Anything of interest to your children can give cause for celebrations: the first tooth lost, the first snow, the last day of school, learning to ride a bike, winning an award, the first day of entering his or her teens, or whatever strikes your fancy.

One mom, on the same day every summer, takes her kids to a children's museum in a nearby city to see the rock and space exhibits. Another family visits Estes Park in the Colorado mountains every Fourth of July week, another explores caves, another keeps the same camping date every year. One family stays home on Halloween and has its own "Hallelujah party" in the basement by dressing up in costumes of Bible characters and playing games.

Lib's five grown children and all their kids travel from various states to meet at a North Carolina coastal resort on the same week in July every year. They use the occasion to celebrate birthdays that have occurred in the first half of the year. The other family birthdays are observed when they all meet at her Kentucky home for New Year's Day.

Traditions help preserve memories. These are things we do habitually every year, things we teach our children and pass on to them. Telling stories from our own childhood, or sharing legends from our parents' or grandparents' lives, can be fun and entertaining. Most importantly we can pass on to our children our Christian values, roots, and heritage.

Making Happy Memories

One mom wrote that when her daughter, Nicole, was in her early teens, she developed a real interest in professional baseball—

particularly the Atlanta Braves. "No one in our family had ever been interested in sports, but we decided the whole family, including the younger children, would watch the Braves' games on television together," she said. "We listened as Nicole recited endless statistics about her favorite players, and we took her to the mall to get autographs. Going from our home in Florida to our first Braves game in the Atlanta stadium was exciting for all of us. We have great memories that will last a lifetime."

While you may not have teens in your household yet, when you do, you may find you'll need to adjust your usual schedule to enjoy some family time together. Christina and her husband have a seven-year-old and two teenagers.

"Tom and Heidi, our high schoolers, sometimes show up in our bedroom around 10:00 P.M. and pounce on the bed," she wrote. "Even though we may be tired, we don't kick them out. Some wonderful memories have been made during these late evenings. On weekend nights Eric joins the crowd and all five of us have fun talking while propped up in our bed. My husband and I may have been up since 5:00 A.M., but we ask God to replenish our strength, and he always does."

For years Marilyn and her family enjoyed late afternoon pic-nics on summer weekends at Jones Beach outside New York City. An Italian who loved to cook, she always made lots of thick hero sandwiches loaded with eggplant parmesan. Her husband and four kids never wanted her to vary the menu. They'd leave home by car by at least 3:00 P.M. on a weekend afternoon and by the time they arrived at the beach, the weather was cooler and they had avoided the crowds.

In the winter, right after church on Sundays, they'd gather up their ice skates and head for an open pond in a New York park. For years this was a family ritual. "The kids still talk about all the fun they used to have then, either ice skating or going to the beach," Marilyn said. "Really, I didn't know we were making such wonderful memories for them. We were just trying to do family things together."

Staying Connected with Grandparents

Making a family photo album or scrapbook and staying in close touch with grandparents are fun ways for children to learn about their family history. If you don't have a grandparent close by, you could "adopt" one who attends your church or lives in your neighborhood.

If both you and your parents or in-laws have access to the Internet, it's good to encourage your children to communicate with their grandparents via e-mail. My (Ruthanne's) four grandchildren live thousands of miles away—one in graduate school and three younger ones being homeschooled—but they keep in touch with my husband and me by e-mail much more than they ever did by writing letters.

Roberta, the mother of four young sons, was thrilled when her grandparents moved to her town to be closer to her parents. "Having their grandparents and great-grandparents close by means my sons have six adults to let them know how absolutely awesome they are," she says. "And they offer loving guidance when the kids *aren't* so awesome. All four grandparents know firsthand the prayer needs of my sons, but they also know where the diapers and wipes are at my house.

"My boys never need to wonder what Grandma and Grandpa or Nana and Papa look like," she says. "To them, Grandma is a real person who gives warm kisses and loving hugs and does a great Donald Duck impression. Sometimes when I'm too tired to laugh at my children's jokes, Grandma isn't. My sons have learned to sing 'Have You Ever Gone A-Fishing?' while dancing around Great-Grandaddy (Papa) as he strums his guitar, just as I once did, and my mom before me. What a legacy we have."[3]

Roberta's mom, Mitzi, goes to the elementary school every Friday to eat with her oldest grandson in the cafeteria, and then she stays after lunch to tell the class a story.

Many schools now invite "grandfriends" to participate in class activities. I (Quin) recently received such an invitation as I now have five grandchildren in schools near us. When our pastor's children were in elementary school, my husband and I would attend their Grandparents' Day events as substitutes for their own grandparents who lived in another state. Because we pray for our pastor's family daily, this provided us with deeper understanding of how to pray more effectively for the children.

My (Quin's) sister Ann reads a short story or book during long-distance phone calls to her eight-year-old granddaughter almost every night of the week. Some grandparents read a story into a cassette recorder and then send both the book and the tape to their grandchildren.

Reading into a tape recorder is an idea busy moms can use too. The first time you read the story to your child, just switch on the tape recorder, and if you don't have time the next time she wants to read, pop in the tape. It's not as personal, but it will work. Statistics show that reading to your child can help prepare his brain for mastering language skills.

"There's a clear indication of a neurological difference between kids who have been regularly read to and kids who have not," says one child health expert.[4] He also suggests that parents and caregivers interact verbally with children whenever possible.

I (Quin) continually read to my grandkids. I sometimes write them notes telling funny stories about their parents but I also relate some of their sterling qualities. I answer questions such as: What was Daddy like when he was little? What was Mom's favorite food, music, or subject in school?

This past Christmas I gave the six grandchildren velveteen "treasure boxes" containing books appropriate for their ages, prayers I wrote for them for now and the future, and a personal letter reviewing the past year and expressing my pride in their accomplishments. I enclosed a small amount of money in each note for them to put in their "travel jar." Our goal is to see that each of them takes a trip to Israel someday.

My daughter-in-law, Dana, often reads aloud from some of the books I've given her three children. She also gets up at 6:30 A.M. to have a devotional time with her eight-year-old, Kara, before she awakens the younger two. Their "mommy and daughter" moments have become a special bonding time.

Two Extreme Personalities

Often a mom has to take into consideration the unique personalities of her children as she prays for ways to best connect with each one. JoEllen has one daughter who is quiet and painfully shy, while her preschooler is gregarious and outgoing.

Eight-year-old Karen enjoys sports that don't require much interaction, such as horseback riding or swimming. She is also a bookworm who loves to read in every spare moment. On the other hand, Leslie, the three-year-old, is vivacious, lively, never meets a stranger, and has little sense of fear. Hence, her mom must continually remind her she can't trust everyone who stops to speak to her.

"Of course it's easier to deal with a child with a winning, bubbly personality," says JoEllen. "But I go out of my way every day to have one-on-one time with shy Karen so she feels affirmed. I tell her wonderful stories of her babyhood as we look through picture albums and laugh together, and each day I try to find something to compliment her about. I also look for ways to draw her out and help her to be more comfortable around people."

At night JoEllen or her husband reads Bible stories to the girls and encourages them to pray. "Our mealtime prayers seem to last a long time when we let the girls do the praying, yet we don't mind," she says. "One thing we insist on is making holidays special—celebrating the true meaning of Easter and Christmas and finding ways to make the girls' birthdays memorable."

Children desperately need to hear their parents' words of love, affirmation, affection, and appreciation to help counter the many negative influences they face each day. Finding ways to help bring out the best in your kids and to have fun times together are almost limitless. Here are some ideas you may want to consider:

- Save on parties by finding other ways to honor your child. One mother who grew tired of having a dozen kids over for her son's birthday party gave her child a choice of two different amusement parks he could go to with his family, and she let him choose only one friend to go along. The refreshments, birthday cake, and presents were enjoyed in the picnic area after petting llamas, riding a donkey, and soaring high in a child-size ferris wheel. "It was my best birthday ever," he told his mom that night.

- Encourage children to make their own cards and gifts for others.

- Find ways to stir up creativity in your children. One 13-year-old made beaded jewelry and sold it to pay part of her way to music camp. She had fun in the process of creating something, besides the joy of knowing she had contributed to her camp expenses.

- Teach your children to work for their "rewards"—the extras they want but that are out of reach of your family budget. Do work projects as a family.

- Bake bread together. Get involved in kneading the dough, rolling it out, shaping it, and, of course, eating it. Or make cookies to decorate and share with friends, grandparents, or other relatives.

- Visit a radio or television station, or your city newspaper office (phone ahead and make arrangements). Then let the children reenact their own version of a show at home, or write a sample newspaper article about one of their events at school or church.

❧ If you have a video camera, let the kids put together their own video show. It can involve pets, other kids, a family vacation, or be a documentary of something significant in your community.

❧ Let the kids plan a special picnic—from going to the grocery store with you to buy the food to preparing it, packing it, and even setting up the table when you arrive at the picnic site they help to choose.

Add your own ideas to these and exchange some with other moms.

When our (Quin's) children were growing up, we had a large poster of the following motto framed above our kitchen table. We read it often before we ate our evening meal. I still love the words it expresses for our family.

God Made Us a Family
We need one another.
We love one another.
We forgive one another.
We work together.
We play together.
We worship together.
Together we use God's Word.
Together we grow in Christ.
Together we love all men.
Together we serve our God.
Together we hope for heaven.
These are our hopes and ideas;
Help us to attain them, O God;
Through Jesus Christ our Lord, amen.[5]

Prayer

Lord, thank you that you put us in families. Show us how to affirm each child and make each one feel accepted, and how to have more fun times together. Give us creative ideas for building happy memories for our children that will last a lifetime. Thank you for giving us the Word of God, a wonderful book of "remembrances." Amen.

Scriptures for Meditation

"You will show me the path of life; in Your presence is fullness of joy; at Your right hand are pleasures forevermore" (Psalm 16:11 NKJV).

"Sing joyfully to the LORD, you righteous; it is fitting for the upright to praise him...Sing to him a new song; play skillfully and shout for joy" (Psalm 33:1,3).

"A happy heart is good medicine and a cheerful mind works healing" (Proverbs 17:22 AMP).

"Nehemiah said, 'Go and enjoy choice food and sweet drinks, and send some to those who have nothing prepared. This day is sacred to our Lord. Do not grieve, for the joy of the Lord is your strength'" (Nehemiah 8:10).

"If you obey my commands, you will remain in my love, just as I have obeyed my Father's commands and remain in his love. I have told you this so that my joy may be in you and that your joy may be complete" (John 15:10-11).

"And the disciples were filled with joy and with the Holy Spirit" (Acts 13:52).

12
Power to Launch
Them into Adulthood

Finding God's Vision for Your Children's Future

Let us hold unswervingly to the hope we profess,
for he who promised is faithful.
—HEBREWS 10:23

Years ago when I became a mother, I began an inner journey that
has revolutionized my life. I began a journey to my heart. As I cared
for my two daughters, I came to see that my children—with their
love, neediness, and daily demands—were shaping me in ways I but
dimly perceived...Because of my daughters I have become more
patient, hopeful, accepting, and less perfectionistic.

I, in turn, have shaped my children's lives, molding their sense of
self, their values, and their conscience, as well as their feelings about
intimacy. In short, I have touched their very souls. Such is the
wonder and power of mother love.[1]
—DR. BRENDA HUNTER

Spirit-led mom needs the enabling power of the Holy
Spirit for every season of motherhood she experiences. But she especially needs it when one of her offspring is about to leave home and be launched into adulthood.
From the time they are born, we know our children eventually will leave the nest and live independently from Mom and

Dad. But knowing it, and feeling we've prepared them for this reality, are two different things.

God Has a Plan

As we compiled a list of "things to do" to prepare your child for the future, the moms who shared with us said they did most or all of these:

- assured their children that they are loved unconditionally

- talked about Jesus and his salvation promise to them from an early age on

- prayed with them, and taught them to pray and always talk to God about their problems

- took them to church regularly, including youth events

- attended their school and extracurricular activities as often as possible

- became well acquainted with their friends

- got them involved in "family time" togetherness when possible

- helped them learn responsibility by assigning appropriate duties and chores

- tried to be fair and consistent in applying discipline

- helped them learn how to handle money responsibly

- tried to instill Christian values in them by being a good example

- provided them with the best affordable education

Probably no parent could score 100 percent on such a checklist, but as we stay focused on God in our efforts, he can redeem our mistakes and help us to improve. His strength can enable us to learn through our experiences in every difficulty and help us to encourage others along the way.

"God has a plan and a purpose for your life," I (Quin) often said to my children when they were young. My husband and I felt it was essential for them to grasp this idea early on. Later, when one of our daughters was a college senior, she heard a pastor say the same thing, but he added, "It's your job to find out what that purpose is and do it!" That proved to be a pivotal point in her life as she wept before the Lord and asked him to show her what it was. After graduation she enrolled in Bible school to prepare for overseas ministry.

When Kathleen, now the mother of five children, attended a Christian college, she had no idea her Bible classes would later prove a valuable source of strength to her as a mom.

"God's Word deposited in my spirit gave me a strong biblical foundation," she said. "I later heard that memorizing Scripture can be compared to preserving or canning food for the winter. I've found that not only do those stored-up Bible verses provide what I need now in rearing my children and preparing them for the future, they supplied comfort when we lost our eight-year-old son to cancer. God used His Word to help see us through."

Kathleen says she asks the Holy Spirit for guidance, direction, and strength all through the day in looking after her family and working part-time in her husband's business.

"I'm working on not being such a perfectionist and not nagging my kids so much—especially about cleaning up their rooms. But I do take away privileges if they don't do their regular chores. Caring for the animals and mowing the acreage around our house is helping them grow into responsible kids who will be better prepared for adulthood."

Mary Elizabeth is a mom who learned she could trust God to help her launch her children into their future by providing the training they needed for their various careers. But it meant yielding to the Holy Spirit's guidance, even when it ran counter to her own plans.

God's Promise of Provision

"Over the years I've found that if I have a word from the Lord—whether from the Bible or one he speaks to my heart—I can make it through just about anything," Mary Elizabeth told us.

Because she was concerned about providing a college education for her five children, she fully planned to return to her nursing career to help pay the tuition bills. But every time she determined to go back to work, she'd find out she was pregnant again. In the meantime, she became a crossing guard for a school in order to be at home with her children and still earn a bit of extra income.

"One day as I was talking to the Lord, he spoke to me very clearly," she said. "He asked me to give him my desire for a nursing career and stay at home to mother my children, keeping them covered with prayer. I didn't see how I could not work. But I felt he showed me that each child had a special calling, and he wanted me to teach them and pray for them to enter into his plan for their lives. If I would do this, he would fully provide for them to go to college."

Mary Elizabeth obeyed the Lord and her husband gave her his full support. But sure enough, the storms of doubt and guilt hit with a fury. Esther, her oldest, enrolled in a Christian college, which would help her prepare for her dream of being an overseas missionary. She had some scholarships, but a balance of $4300 was due to be paid in a few short weeks.

"I knew the Lord had promised *full provision*, but we barely had enough money for household expenses, much less for college tuition," Mary Elizabeth said. "Esther was becoming increasingly frustrated and upset and wondering if I had really heard from the Lord at all. I would retreat to my room to seek God and read again the word he had given me years before to regain strength for the battle.

"About ten days before it was time to take Esther to college, we learned she had won a $4300 grant for her first year's tuition. This amount, exactly what we lacked, was being sent directly to the school. Through the years since that victory, God has faithfully provided for all our children's education as they have prepared to serve him in missions. God has been true to his Word."[2]

Because she's had kids in college for the past 13 years, Mary Elizabeth has had to come to a place of complete trust in God's provision. And as she has learned to trust him, so have her husband and children. The older ones now serve on various mission fields, and her youngest has graduated from nursing school and ministers with her doctor husband in the inner city. Now this mom's focus is on praying for all her children and their spouses in their places of service.

Persist with God's Love

When I (Quin) recently visited my long-time prayer-partner and mentor, Fran Ewing, I asked her what advice she would give young moms today. This was her response:

> Loving the Lord puts you in a position to receive God's love. You can't give what you don't have. But God's love flowing through you makes for a loving mom who can endure the present trials with her eye on the future. Every trial has an ending, so it's important to have the long view and not just focus on the situation at the moment.
>
> We can depend on God to give us the grace, desire, and power to do his will, even in tough places. We must decide that we will invest in our children and

their future, and declare, "I will lay down my life for them. I am going to love and parent these children, and, with God's help, lay aside my own desires for his desires and purposes. I am not quitting!"

We've talked with a lot of moms who determine that no matter how deep the trouble their kids find themselves in, they will intercede in prayer until a turnaround occurs. In our next story, you'll meet a mother who had tried to be the best mom she knew how to be, but she still saw her daughter's life go into a downward spiral. Refusing to believe the dark predictions for her child's future, she took action through prayer and intervention to see her teen's life put back on track.

A Battle with Drugs

Rita was shocked when she learned that 17-year-old Joanie was experimenting with drugs, but she was even more dismayed to find out Joanie was getting her supply through kids at the Christian school she attended. The school administrators, who flatly denied there was a drug problem on their campus, offered her no support.

Not only did Rita pray a lot, asking God to help her and her daughter through this, she did research and became proactive in addressing the problem. Because Joanie's grades were so low, it appeared she would not even graduate. Rita appealed to the academic committee to allow her daughter to graduate, and they finally agreed. One said, "It's obvious she will never go to college anyway."

This determined mom set aside a day to go up on a mountain overlooking their city to fast and pray for Joanie. Her specific prayer was: "God, open her eyes and open her ears so that she will see and hear evil and be quick to run from it."

Later that night—at 2:00 A.M.—Joanie called home on her cell phone. "Mom, I'm so sorry, so sorry…" she said breathlessly. "I don't think I'll make it home. I may never see you again."

Rita offered to come get her, but Joanie insisted it was too dangerous, saying she had to keep running from the evil men who were chasing her. Then she ran all the way to her cousin's apartment, who took one look at her and rushed her to the emergency room. The doctor who treated her told her plainly, "You are going to die if you stay on the road you're on now."

Joanie never told her mom about the events of that night except to say she had heard an audible voice telling her, "Get away. Run as fast as you can." Rita is convinced it was the Holy Spirit's warning in answer to her prayers.

Soon after this, when mother and daughter attended a youth rally together, Joanie's heart began turning toward God once more. She graduated from high school and then moved several hundred miles from home to attend Bible school.

"The minute she walked across that campus, something miraculous happened. She was instantly delivered from her craving for drugs," Rita reports.

With her faith renewed and her heart firmly rooted in God's Word, Joanie returned home a year later and enrolled in a Christian college. She has now finished two years and hopes to pursue work in the medical field so that she can help others.

As a young mom, you don't need to fear the teen years, but it helps if you make up your mind ahead of time that you will stand in prayer for your kids through whatever trials and temptations may come. That's what Rita did, and that's the kind of resolve we see in this next story.

Depending Totally on God

Gloria and her husband, a pastor, raised their four sons in church and had high hopes for their future. But by the time the boys were in their early teens, they learned that three of them were addicted to drugs or alcohol. The youngest son decided he didn't want to follow his brothers' example. Instead, he embraced an Eastern religion.

Her "far-out" children were anything but models for other youth in the church, but Gloria's main concern was to see them become godly, responsible young men.

"When your world is totally chaotic, you discover that you must totally depend on God for wisdom," she said. "You have no control over others' choices, so you have to lean into the Lord even more. Crises, I've discovered, drive you closer to Christ." How did she face the pressures? She tells us in her own words:

- I joined a support group for parents who had children with problems like mine. As I began to overcome guilt, this group helped me regain my dignity as a person.

- I played Christian worship music all day long, both in my kitchen and in my sons' rooms. I focused on who God is and not on how my boys were acting out.

- Knowing my children had been dedicated to the Lord and raised on the Bible, I clung to the passage that says God's Word will not return void (see Isaiah 55:11). I knew that someday they'd come back to their Christian roots. Waiting was the hard part, especially on days when they were rebellious or lashed out at me in rage.

- I didn't focus only on the now, but on their futures. I prayed about their choices, including godly mates for each one, and careers suited to each one's talents and personalities.

- I declared to God that nothing could change my relationship with him—not even if one of my boys died. I loved and worshiped God for who he is, and I was determined that he would come first in my life.

- I was persistent in prayer. I prayed the Scriptures for my sons, declaring God's promises for our family. I dug deeper and deeper into the Bible.

⚡ I enlisted two faithful friends to pray with me regularly over the phone. They could identify with my "mom prayers" and became my strong encouragers. I could call them anytime and they'd pray right then.

⚡ We maintained an "open door" so the boys knew they could come home when they needed to and we would receive them.

Gloria remembers the day a bedraggled son, pencil thin and wearing unkempt dreadlocks, knocked on her door. She hardly recognized him. "Help me, Mom. I need help," he begged. She and her husband once again admitted him to a drug rehabilitation center. Another son was picked up for drug possession and spent the night in jail, but he called his mother from there to say, "Mom, God's got my attention now."

God intervened in each of their lives, and today all four sons are serving the Lord and have a loving relationship with their parents. Years of Gloria's persistence in prayer and trusting the help of the Holy Spirit made all the difference for this family.

Tenacious Trust and Boldness

Like Rita and Gloria, each of us will face experiences when our best efforts seem to be in vain and our faith could easily waver. I (Ruthanne) can look back on times when I prayed about a situation with one of our children, only to see matters become worse instead of better. It would have been easy to give up on prayer, which of course the enemy tempted me to do.

But I have to keep my trust in a God who is able to take what the devil intends for evil and turn it into something good. I've learned the value of persisting in prayer no matter how discouraging the circumstances. At such times I make this declaration. You may want to make it too:

Lord, I don't understand the things that are happening in the natural realm regarding this situation with my child. But I choose to believe that you are working in the spiritual realm in ways I cannot see. I know your power is greater than all the power of the enemy. Your Word declares in James 5:16 that the prayer of a righteous person is powerful and effective, and I am righteous because of the blood of Jesus. Therefore, I continue to stand in faith and trust you to do the maximum to bring glory and honor to your Son in my child's life.

As I (Quin) mentioned earlier, my husband and I fought a five-year battle in prayer using Scripture promises to see our three children come back from the land of the enemy. What if we had quit praying in just two years, or three? Persistence means having a singleness of purpose or tenacity in trusting God's promises. That's what we clung to day after discouraging day until we saw victory.

One of our favorite parables in the Bible is Luke 11:5-13, where Jesus tells of a man who knocks on his friend's door at midnight asking for three loaves of bread for his unexpected guests. The friend tells him to go away and refuses to get up, but the man keeps on knocking. Because of his tenacity, his friend finally gets up and gives him as much as he wants.

Jesus concludes, "So I say to you: Ask and it will be given to you; seek and you will find; knock and the door will be opened to you. For everyone who asks receives; he who seeks finds; and to him who knocks, the door will be opened" (Luke 11:9-10).

In other words, he is teaching us to be persistent, bold, and specific in asking him to answer our prayers.

Praying with a Friend

"I have a new heart for heartache because of the trials I've been through," said Sherri, a pastor's wife in a large metropolitan church. "I've learned there is usually another woman in your church who is struggling with a similar problem. If you need encouragement, go to an encourager. If you have a rebellious child, go to a mom who prayed hers through to victory. We need to humble ourselves and ask someone else to pray with us and speak into our lives."

Prayer partners do strengthen you. If your husband will pray with you, that's great. Together you can build a spiritual intimacy as you yield to the Holy Spirit's leading. But let's be realistic. Not all husbands are willing, or will take the time, to pray with their wives. So ask God for just the right woman friend to become your prayer partner. Those who pray together should have shared concerns, similar goals, and a common focus.

Here are some guidelines to follow in praying with a prayer partner:

- Have a specific time to pray and commit to it. I (Quin) prayed on the phone with my best friend Lib for five minutes at 8:00 A.M. every weekday for many years. Our prayer focus was our children. We started when we had kids still in diapers and continued even after they left for college. Later, when I moved, I met for three years with five other women for one hour at 5:30 every Monday morning. Our prayer emphasis was our families.

- Set a time limit. Please don't neglect your family by spending too much prayer time with your friend. Find a balance and keep priorities. Many women these days exchange prayer requests via e-mail.

- Be considerate and don't hog all the prayer time. Give others a chance to pray too.

- Maintain transparency, confidentiality, humility, and forgiveness.

   ❧ Guard against judgment, idle chitchat, or gossip. Pray; don't discuss the issues.

   ❧ Choose a prayer partner who likes your children and is sympathetic toward your family.

   ❧ Establish your purpose for prayer. Keep it focused.[3]

Jesus said, "If two of you on earth agree about anything you ask for, it will be done for you by my Father in heaven. For where two or three come together in my name, there am I with them" (Matthew 18:19-20).

Jesus always was in agreement with his heavenly Father. In like manner, we should ask the Lord for his will about a situation and then pray in agreement—or "with one mind"—with a prayer partner until we see results. We especially need partners who know the Word, are willing to hear the Holy Spirit's direction, and can agree on a focus. Ideally, they will remain steadfast and pray with us until breakthrough and beyond.

Standing Through the Storms

Every Spirit-led mom eventually will release her children to follow God's leading while she watches from the sidelines and continues to pray for them. This process of becoming a Spirit-led mom takes on deeper dimensions as we learn to lean more and more on Christ and thank him for the storms he has brought us through in the past.

Sometimes the hardest part is watching our children go through storms of their own as they learn to put their trust in the Lord. Author William Gurnall suggests that one reason God doesn't always deliver us from the storm as soon as we would like is to give our faith the opportunity to grow stronger. He uses the analogy of learning to walk:

> When a mother is teaching her child to walk, she stands back a short distance and holds out her hands

to the child, beckoning him to come. Now if she exercises her strength to go to her little one, the child is ill-served, for his unsteady legs are denied the practice they need. If she loves him, she will let him suffer a little at present to ensure his future health. Just so, because God loves His children, He sometimes lets them struggle to strengthen the legs of their unsteady faith.[4]

How hard it is for us to see our children struggle! But isn't that how we got where we are in our own Christian walk? As we floundered to become steady on our feet, God was there holding out his hand all along. And we can trust him to do the same for our children as we launch them into adulthood.

His Power Is Always Available

We have seen throughout this book how moms can rely on the Holy Spirit to help them in their demanding role of motherhood. We have learned that:

- We need the help of the Holy Spirit to rear our children to be responsible, loving adults as well as influential servants of God.

- Through his guidance we can overcome our fears and find peace that lasts.

- Our weaknesses can become strengths as we learn to depend more fully on God's power to help us.

- He can show us how to establish godly boundaries and discipline with love.

- He can handle all our "what-if's" and heal our guilt.

- He can give us wisdom and discernment for reaching and teaching each child.

❧ He can help us to forgive our family members and our-selves.

❧ During times of pressure, he helps calm our frantic pace.

❧ He can provide physical and emotional well-being for our family members.

❧ He can equip us to mentor our children and help them build a life of faith.

❧ By embracing the joy of the Lord, we can enjoy life as a family.

❧ Through persistence and prayer, we can see our children fulfill their purpose in life.

You may begin your journey as a mom wondering how you will ever fulfill the enormous responsibility God has entrusted to you. But with the Holy Spirit as your helper to give you wisdom step-by-step, you *can* meet the challenge and also find joy in the journey. Before you know it, your children will be preparing to leave the nest and you'll be asking yourself how the years could have flown by so quickly.

But no matter how tall they grow, how many mistakes they make, how mature they become, how many heartaches they suffer, or how many accomplishments they achieve, you will never stop being a mom. Forever you will be grateful to God for his faithfulness to you and your children, and always you will have wonderful memories to treasure in your heart.

Prayer

Thank you, Lord, for your faithfulness to me over the years. I count my blessings as I see your intervention in many situations I thought were hopeless. Continue to give me your strength and wisdom to raise my children to follow your will. When I look at the storms instead of seeing your greatness, draw me back to your presence. You are an awesome God, a faithful Father. Thank you so much for sending the Holy Spirit to teach me how to become a better mom. I love you, Lord. Amen.

Scriptures for Meditation

"Joseph told them...As far as I am concerned, God turned into good what you meant for evil, for he brought me to this high position I have today so that I could save the lives of many people'" (Genesis 50:19-20 TLB).

"As it is written: 'No eye has seen, no ear has heard, no mind has conceived what God has prepared for those who love him.' But God has revealed it to us by his Spirit" (1 Corinthians 2:9-10).

"For our light and momentary troubles are achieving for us an eternal glory that far outweighs them all. So we fix our eyes not on what is seen, but on what is unseen. For what is seen is temporary, but what is unseen is eternal" (2 Corinthians 4:17-18).

"Let us not lose heart and grow weary and faint in acting nobly and doing right, for in due time and at the appointed season we shall reap, if we do not loosen and relax our courage and faint" (Galatians 6:9 AMP).

"So do not throw away your confidence; it will be richly rewarded. You need to persevere so that when you have done the will of God, you will receive what he has promised" (Hebrews 10:35-36).

"Wait and hope for and expect the Lord: be brave and of good courage and let your heart be stout and enduring. Yes, wait for and hope for and expect the Lord" (Psalm 27:14 AMP).

APPENDIX

Learning to Pray the Scriptures

I (Quin) admit it. As a young mom, my prayers were more crisis based than belief based. When my children were sick, I tried to bargain with God. You should have heard what I'd promise him, not knowing that this wasn't exactly scriptural. Mostly I prayed general "bless us" prayers for my little family.

Then one night while kneeling in a pastor's office, I invited the Holy Spirit to come be my teacher. I found that I had to invite his presence daily. Then, too, I had to prepare my heart by confessing any unforgiveness, judgmental attitudes, disappointment, anxiety, unbelief, or anything else that came to mind that was displeasing to God. It was also helpful to praise and worship him for who he is, not just for what he had done for me.

As I searched the Scriptures for ways to pray more effectively I discovered these keys: Be open to the Holy Spirit. When you don't know exactly what to say when you pray, ask God to show you. He may drop a Scripture verse or an idea into your mind, or even have another person say something to you that relates directly to your prayer concern (see Romans 8:26-27).

You will find these are very practical guidelines:

- ⚹ Be specific. When Jesus asked the blind man what he wanted him to do for him, he answered, "that I may receive my sight" (Mark 10:51 NKJV). So we can pray explicit prayers.

- ⚹ Be persistent. It's always too soon to stop praying. Jesus tells a parable that encourages us to be bold and persistent to "ask, seek, knock" which is a continuous asking, seeking, knocking (see Luke 11:9-10).

⯎ Be in agreement with a prayer partner or prayer support team (see Matthew 18:19).

⯎ Be Bible based. As we get better acquainted with the Bible, we grow to know God more intimately and we begin to understand how to pray in accordance with his will.

Often a Bible verse says exactly what we want to say, so we paraphrase it and make it our prayer. For example:

> "I thank you, Lord, that you know the plans you have for my child (name) are to prosper her and not to harm her, plans to give her hope and a future" (see Jeremiah 29:11).

> "I pray that you, O Lord, will give your angels charge over my children, to guard them in all their ways" (see Psalm 91:11).

> "Lord, I pray that my child (name) may prosper in all things and be in health, just as his soul prospers" (see 3 John 2 NKJV).

> "Our Father in heaven...may your kingdom come, your will be done in my children's lives...lead them not into temptation, but deliver them from the evil one" (see Matthew 6:9-10,13).

> "God, grant (name) repentance that leads to the knowledge of the truth that he may come to his senses and escape from the snare of the devil, having been held captive by him to do his will" (2 Timothy 2:25-26 NASB).

Here are scriptural goals you may want to incorporate in your prayers for your children:

- 🐌 That Jesus Christ be formed in them (see Galatians 4:19).

- 🐌 That they—the seed of the righteous—will be delivered from the evil one (see Proverbs 11:21 KJV; Matthew 6:13).

- 🐌 That they will be taught of the Lord and their peace will be great (see Isaiah 54:13).

- 🐌 That they will train themselves to discern good from evil and have a good conscience toward God (see Hebrews 5:14; 1 Peter 3:21).

- 🐌 That God's laws will be in their minds and on their hearts (see Hebrews 8:10).

- 🐌 That they will choose companions who are wise—not fools—being neither sexually immoral, drunkards, idolaters, slanderers, nor swindlers (see Proverbs 13:20; 1 Corinthians 5:11).

- 🐌 That they will remain sexually pure and keep themselves only for their spouse, asking for God's grace to keep such a commitment (see Ephesians 5:3,31,33).

- 🐌 That they will honor their parents (see Ephesians 6:1-3).[1]

It's a good idea now, while your children are young, to plant "waiting prayers" for their future. I learned this from a mom who wrote her prayers on egg-shaped pieces of paper and slipped them into her Bible. Her petition was, "Lord, please hatch these prayers in your perfect timing." Years later she rejoiced over the wonderful fruit in her children's lives that came in answer to those waiting prayers.

Remember, the wise gardener plants tiny seeds, but then she has the good sense not to dig them up every few days to see if a crop is on the way. So we may need to wait for God to bring answers to our prayers in his timing. But we have planted good seeds, and in faith we continue to water them with Scripture, prayers, promises, and praise. Then we wait expectantly for the day the Creator brings forth a good harvest, "for he who promised is faithful" (Hebrews 10:23).

NOTES

Chapter 1—I Can't Do This Alone

1. Elizabeth George, *Life Management for Busy Women* (Eugene, OR: Harvest House Publishers, 2002), p. 99.

2. "He Giveth More Grace," by Annie Johnson Flint, © 1941, Lillenas Publishing Company, (administered by The Copyright Company, Nashville, TN). All rights reserved. International copyright secured. Used by permission.

3. Tomato Cards, DCI Studios.

4. From the *Census Bureau News*, June 2001, U.S. Census Bureau Public Information Office, Washington, D.C.

5. Glenda Malmin, *The Journey of a Mother's Heart* (Ventura, CA: Regal Books, 1999), p. 7.

Chapter 2—Power for Your Fears

1. Lisa Bevere, *Out of Control and Loving It* (Lake Mary, FL: Charisma House, 1996), p. 106.

2. Max Lucado, *Traveling Light* (Colorado Springs: Waterbrook, 2001), p. 49.

3. Adapted from Quin Sherrer and Ruthanne Garlock, *A Woman's Guide to Breaking Bondages*, (Ann Arbor, MI: Servant Publications, 1994), pp. 102-06.

4. Kathe Wunnenberg, *Grieving the Loss of a Loved One* (Grand Rapids, MI: Zondervan, 2000), pp. 148-50, 119. Used by permission.

Chapter 3—Power for Your Weaknesses and Strengths

1. Miriam Neff, *Sisters of the Heart* (Nashville: Thomas Nelson, 1995), pp. 27-28.

2. Herbert Lockyer, *All About the Holy Spirit* (Peabody, MA: Hendrickson, 1995), pp. 106-07. [This work was first published as *The Breath of God* in 1949 by Union Gospel Press.]

3. Lisa Bevere, *Out of Control and Loving It* (Lake Mary, FL: Charisma House, 1996), p. 124.

4. Ibid., p. 125.

5. Ibid., p. 126.

6. Elizabeth Sherrill, *All the Way to Heaven* (Grand Rapids, MI: Fleming H. Revell, 2002), pp. 129-30.

7. Susan Goodwin Graham, "Anne Graham Lotz: In Heavenly Places," in *LifeWise*, October-November 2002, pp. 9-10.

Chapter 4—Power to Discipline with Love

1. Teresa A. Langston, *Parenting Without Pressure* (Colorado Springs: Pinion Press, 2001), pp. 47-48.

2. *Nelson's Illustrated Bible Dictionary* (Thomas Nelson Publishers 1986, PC Study Bible Ver. 30c New Reference Library, CD Rom).

3. Langston, *Parenting Without Pressure*, p. 48.

4. Brenda Armstrong, *The Single Mom's Workplace Survival Guide* (Ann Arbor, MI: Servant Publications, 2002), p. 82.

5. Kevin Leman, *Making Children Mind Without Losing Yours* (Grand Rapids, MI: Fleming H. Revell, 2002), pp. 106, 110, 113.

6. Adapted from Sandra P. Aldrich, *From One Single Mother to Another* (Ventura, CA: Regal Books, 1991), pp. 126-28. Used by permission.

7. Ross Campbell, M.D., *How to Really Love Your Child* (Colorado Springs: Victor Books, 1992), p. 121.

8. Ibid., p. 120.

9. Ibid., p. 122.

Chapter 5—Power for Your "If Onlys"

1. R.T. Kendall, "When You Can't Forgive Yourself," in *SpiritLed Woman*, December-January 2002-2003, p. 26. (Magazine article adapted from R.T. Kendall's book, *Total Forgiveness*, Lake Mary, FL: Charisma House, 2002).

2. Ibid., pp. 26-27.

3. Adapted from Quin Sherrer with Ruthanne Garlock, *How to Pray for Your Children* (Ventura, CA: Regal Books, 1998), pp. 99-101. Used with permission.

4. James C. Dobson, *Parenting Isn't for Cowards* (Dallas: Word Publishing, 1987), p. 42.

Chapter 6—Power to Find Answers

1. Elisa Morgan, *Mom to Mom* (Grand Rapids, MI: Zondervan, 1996), p. 33.

2. "Homeschooling Research," from the website of the Home School Legal Defense Association <www.hslda.org/research/faq>.

Chapter 7—Power to Forgive

1. Joyce Thompson, *Preserving a Righteous Seed* (Dallas: CTM Publishing, 1998), p. 37.

2. Mary Rae Deatrick, *Easing the Pain of Parenthood* (Eugene, OR: Harvest House, 1979), p. 40.

3. Adapted from Debbie Hedstrom, "A Mom's Secret Weapon: Forgiveness," in *Aglow* (December 1987).

4. Corrie ten Boom, *Tramp for the Lord* (Grand Rapids, MI: Fleming H. Revell, 1974), pp. 179-80.

5. Adapted from Quin Sherrer and Ruthanne Garlock, *How to Pray for Your Children* (Ventura, CA: Regal Books, 1998), pp. 167-69, plus a follow-up interview. Used by permission.

6. Ibid., pp. 114-15.

7. W.E. Vine, *An Expository Dictionary of New Testament Words* (Old Tappan, NJ: Fleming H. Revell, 1966), p. 453.

8. Ibid.

Chapter 8—Power for the Pressures of Life

1. Deena Lee Wilson, *A Mom's Legacy* (Ventura, CA: Regal Books, 1991), p. 136.

2. Adapted from Diana Hagee, *The King's Daughter: Becoming the Woman God Created You to Be* (Nashville: Thomas Nelson, 2001), pp. 52, 54.

3. Cheri Fuller, *Quiet Whispers from God's Heart for Women* (Nashville: J. Countryman, 1999), p. 64.

4. Ibid., p. 65.

5. Oswald Chambers, *My Utmost for His Highest*, edited by James Reimann (Grand Rapids, MI: Discovery House, 1992 edition), reading for April 1.

Chapter 9—Power for Healing

1. As quoted in *Stories for a Faithful Heart*, compiled by Alice Gray (Sisters, OR, Multnomah Publishers, 2000), p. 222.

2. Adapted from Quin Sherrer and Ruthanne Garlock, *How to Pray for Your Children* (Ventura, CA: Regal Books, 1998), p. 142. Used by permission.

3. Ibid., pp. 144-45.

Chapter 10—Power to Mentor Your Children

1. Jani Ortlund, *Fearlessly Feminine* (Sisters, OR: Multnomah Publishers, 2000), p. 111.

2. Gloria Gaither, "Those Teachable Moments," in *Moody Monthly*, September 1978, pp. 91-92. As quoted by Anne Ortlund in *Disciplines of the Home* (Dallas: Word Publishing, 1990), p. 125.

3. Adapted from Elisa Morgan, *Mom to Mom* (Grand Rapids, MI: Zondervan, 1996), pp. 85-86.

4. Esther Ilnisky, *Let the Children Pray* (Ventura, CA: Regal Books, 2000), pp. 34, 56.

5. Rachel Burchfield, "Teaching Children to Love the Word of God," in *Signs & Wonders Today*, September 2002, p. 5. Used by permission.

6. Ruth Bell Graham, *Legacy of a Pack Rat* (Nashville: Oliver-Nelson Books, 1989), pp. 98-99.

Chapter 11—Power to Enjoy Life as a Family

1. Edith Schaeffer, *What Is a Family?* (Grand Rapids, MI: Baker Book House, 1975), p. 62.

2. Adapted from Quin Sherrer and Laura Watson, *A Christian Woman's Guide to Hospitality* (Ann Arbor, MI: Servant Publications, 1993), pp. 87-88.

3. Adapted from Quin Sherrer and Ruthanne Garlock, *Grandma, I Need Your Prayers*, (Grand Rapids, MI: Zondervan, 2001), p. 207.

4. "Wired Up," *Focus on Your Child*, p. 2.

5. "The Christian Family Standard," adopted by the Family Life Committee of the Lutheran Church, Missouri Synod. Quoted in *Helping Families Through the Church* (St. Louis: Concordia Publishing, 1957), n.p.

Chapter 12—Power to Launch Them into Adulthood

1. Brenda Hunter, *The Power of Mother Love* (Colorado Springs: Waterbrook, 1997), p. xi.

2. Adapted from Quin Sherrer and Ruthanne Garlock, *A Woman's Guide to Spirit-filled Living* (Ann Arbor, MI: Servant Publications, 1996), pp. 191-92, and recent interviews. Used by permission.

3. Adapted from Quin Sherrer, "Kindred Spirits—Prayer of Agreement," in *PRAY!* December/January 2003, pp. 35-36.

4. William Gurnall, *The Christian in Complete Armour* Volume 1, abridged edition, Ruthanne Garlock, editor (Carlisle, PA: Banner of Truth Trust, 1986), p. 56.

Appendix

1. Adapted from Quin Sherrer and Ruthanne Garlock, *The Spiritual Warrior's Prayer Guide* (Ann Arbor, MI: Servant Publications, 1992), pp. 158-59. Used by permission.

Recommended Reading

Aldrich, Sandra P. *From One Single Mother to Another*. Ventura, CA: Regal Books, 1991.

Barna, George. *Real Teens*. Ventura, CA: Regal Books, 2001.

Barnes, Bob and Emilie. *A Little Book of Manners for Boys*. Eugene, OR: Harvest House, 2000. (Also, *A Little Book of Manners for Girls*.)

Bevere, Lisa. *Out of Control and Loving It!* Lake Mary, FL: Charisma Books, 1996.

Bickel, Bruce and Stan Jantz, *God Is In the Small Stuff and It All Matters*. Uhrichsville, OH: Promise Press, an imprint of Barbour Publishing, 1998.

Brown, Dr. Beth E. *When You're Mom No. 2*. Ann Arbor, MI: Servant Publications, 1991.

Callaway, Phil. *I Used to Have Answers, Now I Have Kids*. Eugene, OR: Harvest House, 2000.

Campbell, Ross, M.D. *How to Really Love Your Child*. Colorado Springs, CO: Chariot Victor, 1992.

Cloud, Henry and John Townsend. *Boundaries with Kids*. Grand Rapids, MI: Zondervan, 1998.

Dobson, James C. *Bringing Up Boys*. Wheaton, IL: Tyndale House, 2001.

Dobson, James C. *Love Must Be Tough*. Waco, TX: Word Books, 1983.

Elliot, Elisabeth, *The Shaping of a Christian Family*. Grand Rapids, MI: Fleming H. Revell, 1992.

George, Elizabeth. *Life Management for Busy Women*. Eugene, OR: Harvest House, 2002.

Hagee, Diana. *The King's Daughter: Becoming the Woman God Created You to Be*. Nashville, TN: Thomas Nelson, 2001.

Hicks, Cynthia and Robert. *The Feminine Journey*. Colorado Springs, CO: NavPress, 1994.

Hunter, Brenda, Ph.D. *The Power of Mother Love*. Colorado Springs, CO: Waterbrook Press, 1997.

Johnson, Barbara. *Splashes of Joy in the Cesspools of Life*. Dallas, TX: Word Publishing, 1992.

Langston, Teresa A. *Parenting Without Pressure*. Colorado Springs, CO: Pinon Press, 2001

Leman, Dr. Kevin. *Making Children Mind Without Losing Yours*. Grand Rapids, MI: Fleming H. Revell, 2000.

Malmin, Glenda. *The Journey of a Mother's Heart*. Ventura, CA: Regal Publishers, 1999.

Marshall, Catherine. *Adventures in Prayer*. Old Tappan, NJ: Chosen Books (distributed by Fleming H. Revell), 1975.

Minirth, Frank B., M.D. and Paul D. Meier, M.D. *Happiness Is a Choice*. Grand Rapids, MI: Baker Book House, 1978, 1991.

Morgan, Elisa. *Mom to Mom*. Grand Rapids, MI: Zondervan, 1996.

Morgan, Elisa and Carol Kuykendall. *Real Moms—Exploding the Myths of Motherhood*. Grand Rapids, MI: Zondervan, 2002.

Neff, Miriam. *Sisters of the Heart*. Nashville, TN: Thomas Nelson, 1995.

Otto, Donna. *Finding a Mentor, Being a Mentor*. Eugene, OR: Harvest House, 2001.

Schaeffer, Edith. *What Is a Family?* Grand Rapids, MI: Baker Book House, 1975, 2000.

Sheets, Dutch. *Tell Your Heart to Beat Again*. Ventura, CA: Regal Books, 2002.

Sheets, Dutch. *Intercessory Prayer*. Ventura, CA: Regal Books, 1996.

Sherrer, Quin, and Ruthanne Garlock. *The Beginner's Guide to Receiving the Holy Spirit*. Ann Arbor, MI: Servant Publications, 2002.

Sherrer, Quin and Ruthanne Garlock. *How to Pray for Your Children*. Ventura, CA: Regal Books, 1998.

Sherrer, Quin and Ruthanne Garlock. *Prayers Women Pray*. Ann Arbor, MI: Servant Publications, 1998.

Sherrer, Quin and Ruthanne Garlock. *Praying Prodigals Home*. Ventura, CA: Regal Books, 2000.

Sherrer, Quin and Ruthanne Garlock. *The Spiritual Warrior's Prayer Guide*. Ann Arbor, MI: Servant Publications, 1992.

Sherrer, Quin and Ruthanne Garlock. *A Woman's Guide to Spiritual Warfare*. Ann Arbor, MI: Servant Publications, 1991.

Sherrer, Quin. *Listen, God Is Speaking to You*. Ann Arbor, MI: Servant Publications, 1999.

Sherrill, Elizabeth. *All the Way to Heaven*. Grand Rapids, MI: Fleming H. Revell, 2002.

Smalley, Gary and John Trent. *The Blessing*. Nashville, TN: Thomas Nelson, 1986.

Smalley, Gary and John Trent. *The Gift of Honor*. Nashville, TN: Thomas Nelson Publishers, 1987.

Smalley, Gary and John Trent. *The Key to Your Child's Heart*. Waco, TX: Word Books, 1984.

Thompson, Joyce. *Preserving a Righteous Seed*. Dallas, TX: CTM Publishing, 1998.

Trent, John. *Be There*. Colorado Springs, CO: Focus on the Family and Waterbook Press, 2000.

Wilkinson, Bruce. *A Life God Rewards*. Sisters, OR: Multnomah, 2002.

Winger, Mell, editor. *Fight on Your Knees*. Colorado Springs, CO: NavPress, 2002.

Wunnenberg, Kathe. *Grieving the Child I Never Knew*. Grand Rapids, MI: Zondervan, 2001.

Wunnenberg, Kathe. *Grieving the Loss of a Loved One*. Grand Rapids, MI: Zondervan, 2000.

Bible Credits

About the Authors

 **Quin Sherrer** is the author of 23 books, 15 of which she coauthored with Ruthanne Garlock. These include the bestselling *How to Pray for Your Children* and *A Woman's Guide to Spiritual Warfare*. Quin and her husband, LeRoy, have three grown children and six grandchildren.

 **Ruthanne Garlock** has coauthored 15 books on prayer and related subjects, and two mission biographies. She is a Bible teacher who often speaks at seminars and women's retreats. Ruthanne and her husband, John, have a blended family of three adult children and four grandchildren.